Elementary Schoolers, Meet Media Literacy

Media, Marketing, and Me Series

Current media literacy and economics books generally approach students as future participants. This book series provides fully developed lessons that address the reality today that children as young as elementary school–age are not only participating in, but are often targets of, the purveyors of persuasive information and goods. This series of lesson books is designed to help teachers train young people to understand the methods and rules of a system of which they are already a part so that young people can emerge better informed and have more awareness and control in their consumption choices. Whether the message comes from commercial peddlers ("You should buy this") or sociopolitical peddlers ("You should believe this"), students need the tools to recognize, deconstruct, and make truly self-aware responses to the ubiquitous "nudges" that will forever be a part of their consumer lives.

Containing explorations in media literacy, behavioral economics, and other social environmental sciences, these hands-on, student-centered activities challenge students to examine the manner and content of information that is disseminated in society, or, to borrow from *The Wizard of Oz*, to see the man behind the curtain even when told to ignore him. Other forthcoming books in the series will be for high school teachers and elementary school teachers.

Elementary Schoolers, Meet Media Literacy

How Teachers Can Bring Economics, Media, and Marketing to Life

Jim Wasserman
David W. Loveland

ROWMAN & LITTLEFIELD
Lanham • Boulder • New York • London

Published by Rowman & Littlefield
An imprint of The Rowman & Littlefield Publishing Group, Inc.
4501 Forbes Boulevard, Suite 200, Lanham, Maryland 20706
www.rowman.com

6 Tinworth Street, London SE11 5AL, United Kingdom

Copyright © 2020 by Jim Wasserman and David W. Loveland

All rights reserved. No part of this book may be reproduced in any form or by any electronic or mechanical means, including information storage and retrieval systems, without written permission from the publisher, except by a reviewer who may quote passages in a review.

British Library Cataloguing in Publication Information Available

Library of Congress Cataloging-in-Publication Data

Names: Wasserman, Jim, 1961– author. | Loveland, David W., 1973– author.
Title: Elementary schoolers, meet media literacy : how teachers can bring economics, media, and marketing to life / Jim Wasserman, David W. Loveland.
Description: Lanham, Maryland : Rowman & Littlefield Publishing Group, 2020. | Series: Media, marketing, & me | Includes bibliographical references and index. | Summary: "This teaching manual supplies lessons designed for elementary students (grades 1–5) that establish a concrete foundation for skill-building in recognizing, deconstructing, evaluating, and choosing for themselves whether to accept a tangible product or intangible message. Students will learn to become active, rather than passive, receivers of messaging, providing a gateway for them to then hone their media literacy skills further as they develop more abstract analytical proficiency."—Provided by publisher.
Identifiers: LCCN 2019038986 (print) | LCCN 2019038987 (ebook) | ISBN 9781475842234 (cloth) | ISBN 9781475842241 (paperback) | ISBN 9781475842258 (epub)
Subjects: LCSH: Media literacy—Study and teaching (Elementary) | Economics—Study and teaching (Elementary) | Marketing—Study and teaching (Elementary)
Classification: LCC P96.M4 W368 2020 (print) | LCC P96.M4 (ebook) | DDC 372.37/4—dc23
LC record available at https://lccn.loc.gov/2019038986
LC ebook record available at https://lccn.loc.gov/2019038987

To our parents, Noa, Doris, Mark, and Janet, for teaching and being role models for us. We know you would be shocked to see us writing books dealing with money matters or effective communication, but really, we were paying attention (mostly).

Contents

Preface ix

1 Can Elementary Students Learn Economics and Media Literacy? 1
2 Marketing and Media: The Twin Pillars of American Society 5
3 Introduction to Basic Economics: The Objective Study of Choice 19
4 Behavioral Economics: How We Are "Nudged" While Making Our Choices 37
5 Coolness: The Super Nudge 55
6 Seeking Media Lit's Holy GRAIL: Consumer Demographics 71
7 An Age-Old Question: Age and Consumerism 91
8 Child's Play or Child's Pay?: Children, Consumerism, and Media 101
9 Media Literacy, Relativity, and Persuasion 119
10 Telling the Truth 139

Glossary 145
Bibliography 151
About the Authors 153

Preface

I owe elementary teachers a long overdue apology.

Many years ago, I was new to teaching, having just come from the world of business litigation. My first school (or rather, the first school willing to have me) was a small private school where staff took on as many roles as needed. So, despite my being hired to teach history to older students, I was asked before I ever set foot in a classroom that I could call my own if I wouldn't mind also taking on an elementary reading and introduction to literature class.

Of course I said yes because I thought, "How hard can teaching elementary kids be, especially compared to my other classes at higher levels?"

Elementary teachers, I apologize.

If there was ever a task that challenged me, that made me both frustrated and eager to take on the task the next day, it was teaching that class.

Like many who are not elementary teachers (and I'm looking at a lot of my colleagues in post-elementary education, here), I assumed that younger childhood education is easier; just make it fun and the kids will do what you say, obedient angels that they are.

The fact is, nothing shows a skilled teacher's prowess better than being able to present ideas and instill skills in a manner appropriate for a young child to enthusiastically take ownership of them.

Over the next twenty-five years of teaching, I taught every grade level from fourth to twelfth, even beyond (including adult classes), but never did I have to take such care in planning as I did when charged with elementary-aged learners (and that includes a career of high school AP courses).

With older students, material often "presents itself" as engaging or relevant, and with the outside pressures of college admission and perhaps the student's intellectual curiosity, the student (hopefully) raises themselves to meet the demands of the coursework. In elementary schools, a teacher is tasked more with bringing the material and child together at the same level, like two halves of a bridge that must meet at exactly the right level lest the entire project fail:

- If the lessons are too focused on *fun*, there is little instilling of foundational skills that the learner will need the rest of their educational career.
- If the lessons are too *boring and rote*, any learning fails to penetrate.

And, of course, there is having to make things age and developmentally appropriate. Most elementary students still think in concrete rather than abstract terms, so notions like "justice" and "honor" can be confusing. This is even more so with the topics of this book—media, economics, and marketing—where not only are many of the ideas abstract (different modes of communication), but there is also the "cruel world" reality that needs to be addressed (some communication is inaccurate, if not dishonest). Tell a high school student that a marketer or politician is not being honest and she will shrug; tell that to an elementary student and her world vision of universal honesty and collaboration may be thrown into upheaval (I know this from my own children).

Fortunately, I had some very good teachers for how to educate young learners in esoteric concepts: the kids themselves. I watched what they did and listened to what they said as they engaged. I then consulted the experts—not the ones who came into the school at the beginning of the year to do a two-hour lecture on how lecturing is bad, but the real experts who every day stand as the only adult in a room where they are the only guard against total chaos breaking out—my fellow (and more seasoned) elementary teachers. I learned how to create a lesson that balanced the students' current need to be engaged with their future need to have acquired some skill or knowledge that will be built upon by future learning.

Student-centered learning. Gamification. Voice and choice. Education consultants proffer so many labels for what almost always comes down to commonsense techniques that teachers in the trenches already know about lesson planning: make it worthwhile, make it appropriate for where the student is (not the teacher), and make it enjoyable.

The lessons in this book are designed with these goals in mind.

The lessons often are related to lessons in our other books for teaching middle- and high-school students (*Middle Schoolers, Meet Media Literacy* and *High Schoolers, Meet Media Literacy*). This is done in order to create an age-appropriate, vertical curriculum of media literacy (of which few schools have any sort) wherein the student re-examines the concepts for reinforcement but with each examination does so in more depth and with more ownership.

The lesson formats are always in four phases we call a Fusion Lesson (yeah, we got a name for ours, too):

1. introductory prompts by the teacher;
2. an activity that is connected to or mirrors the world (often in miniature form);
3. a post-lesson activity to see what observations or conclusions can be drawn;
4. a follow-up investigation of the greater world (usually as homework) for confirmation or modification of their conclusions.

Fusion Lesson

| Introductory questions (lead in) | Activity (student centered) | Post-activity Discussion (lead out) | Expansion & application (student applies as HW) |

For the elementary lessons, the student is given ownership of the activity, while the teacher serves as the "tour guide" through the other three parts. For middle-school lessons, students are charged with taking more command of the post-activity analysis as well, while by high school, the students also then confirm for themselves whether what they observed or concluded in the crucible of the classroom lesson truly applies to the greater world.

I hope that these lessons will be of use to you and, more so, to your students. In a way, elementary teachers are already experts in communication, if not media literacy. The old saying goes that one has not truly mastered a concept until one can adequately explain it to a child, and that is what you do every day.

I learned from the best, starting with that first year of teaching elementary literature. I have used that lesson ever since, no matter what subject or grade level I taught, building my own skills on the solid foundation I gained from my adult time in the elementary classroom.

That, and an everlasting appreciation of *From the Mixed-up Files of Mrs. Basil E. Frankweiler.*

—Jim Wasserman

Chapter One

Can Elementary Students Learn Economics and Media Literacy?

We suppose that, before we dedicate the rest of the book to how to teach elementary children about economics and media literacy, we ought to touch on the question of whether such an endeavor is even possible. (Granted, the rest of the book seems to be a hint as to our point of view, but the issue is worth discussing.)

Economics as a study of wealth systems is fairly abstract. Our entire money system has replaced trading things of concrete value (apples) with things that represent value (money). When one considers the broader definition of economics, that the field is not just about decision making regarding money but about all things in which one must opt for one thing over the other[1] (feeling good about eating apples or guilty about eating cake), it gets even more abstract.

Then there is media literacy. Children are notorious for being too outspoken ("not at this time") and too direct ("don't say that out loud"). When children lie, or even constantly bend and exaggerate the truth, therapists often see it as a sign of deeper issues. (Imagine, then, what such therapists would say to advertisers and politicians judged by the same standards!) Famed developmental psychologist Jean Piaget believed that the ability for abstract reasoning does not develop until the last stage of childhood, known as the *operational stage*, which begins around eleven years old and proceeds into the teen years.

One of us faced such a challenge teaching about nonconcrete notions of integrity and morality in an elementary ethics class. Abstract notions like *fairness* or even *what does it mean to be a good friend?* had to be reduced to manageable "bite sizes." The latter topic, about friendship, is a good example. There, the teacher talked with the students about the phrase "being true blue," with the students learning what the phrase meant and about the various purported origins of the phrase. From there, the class formed a rough definition of their own (someone you can count on to be there for you no matter what). They then were tasked with writing a paragraph about someone in their life they considered "true blue" for them, giving at least two examples of how they were. The paragraphs were read and discussed by the class for trends they saw in who was "true blue" and the kinds of things "true blue" people did.[2] Finally, students were asked to think of ways they could be "true blue" to someone else and an anonymous list of "pledges" was put up on the wall.

Great insight to the complications and gray areas of friendship? Maybe not, but the kids started using the phrase "true blue" (and using it correctly), and years later a couple talked about the lesson and were still using the phrase.

That's one of the toughest parts of being an elementary teacher. If a lesson really works, it may take years to sink in. An old Greek proverb states that "a society grows great when old men plant trees whose shade they know they shall never sit in." We're not saying you teachers are old, or men, but, well, you get the point.

In fact, while non-educators imagine learning as presentation of information leading to an immediate "AHA!" moment, we would suggest that there are two moments of learning that are far more impactful but that can happen long after the lesson, class, or even schooling: the moment of clarity and the moment of confirmation.

THE MOMENT OF CLARITY

Ever read or watch a well-done mystery? As the story builds, the reader/viewer runs through the gamut of emotions: intrigued, confused, misled, frustrated, lost, angry . . . and then it all comes together. Suddenly, all the clues fall into place, the big picture emerges, and the world makes sense (even if there is still a dead body on the floor, ruining the carpet). It's an exhilarating, even empowering feeling!

That's what happens with education. The students don't often get it all. They need more information, more reflection, but at some point, the pieces fall into place and the concept or skill is mastered, at least for a moment. But that moment becomes a gateway to longer moments, then intervals, then consistency.

Education relies on accurate communication, but the subtleties of communication are complex and can be overwhelming to students of all ages, but particularly the younger ones. A student could be overwhelmed by all the ways we communicate—not just what we say, but how we say it, the hedging, the body language, the accompanying visuals, and so on. It's like the student driver being told to check three mirrors; the speedometer; what's in front, back, and on the sides, all at the same time. But at some point it all falls together for the driver, and so our student of communication will say, "I don't buy that pitch" and then explain all the nudges they detect.

THE MOMENT OF CONFIRMATION

Most teachers will tell you that any day can be brightened by a student saying something like, "Remember when we talked about X in class? I saw it after school!" You can see the excitement in the child's eyes that (1) you the teacher know what you are talking about and (2) school is not a total waste of time.

You, of course, have to smile and nod a little, maybe even feign a "Really?!" to allow the child's excitement to bubble on, but inside you know you are doing cartwheels of joy because that student is a little bit more hooked on learning.

That's also a common occurrence with economics and media literacy teaching. The classroom is a lab where many variables are controlled, but almost always a student will return and confirm that what they experienced in the classroom indeed happened in "the real world." With each such instance, the student is retaught the principle, re-enthused about learning, and brought closer to full understanding.

In sum, no, you cannot teach elementary students, with still concrete thinking, all the abstract concepts and intricacies of economics, communication, and media. But then again, you can still teach someone that when you see the tip of an iceberg, they don't have to instantly understand the shape, size, and makeup of that 90 percent of the berg that is unseen and underwater, just that there is danger and to be careful. We are here to help you teach them how to navigate these waters.

NOTES

1. See chapter 2.
2. Moms truly win the "true blue" award by most mentions, although one girl declared her cat true blue for allowing the girl, after a bad day, to dance around with the cat on her head until she felt better.

Chapter Two

Marketing and Media

The Twin Pillars of American Society

A GENERAL (AND GENTLE) INTRODUCTION

When people take flights now, most people give, at best, cursory attention to the pre-flight warnings and instructions, now even done as a movie. What is so amusing about the film, however, is the part where the oxygen mask pops down and the people all calmly react with "Oh, that?" and then quietly place it over their mouths while the airplane is clearly in the midst of a potentially catastrophic danger. Even more so is the child who quietly waits for the parent to secure their own mask before assisting with the child's possible lack of oxygen.[1]

Still, the point is well taken that the adult needs to be in good shape so as to better ensure the well-being of his or her charges. And what is true for a parent with one child on a plane is twenty times more valid for a teacher with twenty (or more) students seeking to take a trip into the worlds of media and economics. Thus, we now present a primer for the teacher to get acquainted with general concepts before assisting their students.

EMPTYING THE CUP

What do you think of when you hear the word "economics"?[2] Lectures on how to spend money wisely? Complex formulas and graphs of supply and demand? Boring professors? Economics is a lot of things, including those (maybe not the boring professors part!), but it is also much more.

Economics is part of your everyday decision making, like should you do lesson planning, take care of family, address all the undone housework, or take some personal sanity restoration time with a book or video game? Will that hot new music group students like be around in another year? What's the best thing for a group of friends to do together this weekend? Even why do we want to hang around with some people but not others? That's all economics, too.

Economics is the study of choice. How do we make choices? What's the best way to make a decision? What factors, including media, influence our decisions?

Now, what do you think of when you hear "media literacy" (or, more commonly, "media lit")? Perhaps the phrase "fake news" jumps to mind, but more generally you get some vague notion of communications studies. Yet you, and even your young students, live amid a swirling ocean of economic and media influences that don't just shape your decisions but actually affect your "independent" decision making as well as how your students act now and who they will grow up to be as people. A good analogy of the impact of media for students to understand is to talk about how fish are not aware of their surrounding water, let alone water quality, yet the water (and its quality) will affect how the fish develops. In the same way, media is all around us, shaping our opinions and decisions now and in the future.

With this manual, you will not only be introduced to the basic economic and media lit concepts that drive this field of study, you will then be able to assist students in learning how to answer questions like those above. Even more, you will not only provide your students with firsthand experience in making economic decisions, but you will also be helping them develop skills of deconstructing "neutral" communication. The media, economic, and financial skills you instill now will lead them to make better choices in the future as they continue to be lifelong consumers of products and information.

With each chapter, we will provide basic explanations of the economic concepts to help you lay the groundwork with your students. Following each section is a series of student-centered lessons that will introduce the concepts by having students explore the world they are in now, rather than giving hypothetical future examples (such as buying a house to learn about interest rates, which few children either understand or relate to). The key is for students to immerse themselves in student-centered activities and then afterward step back and reflect (with your guidance) on what they did, how they felt, what decisions they made, and, most of all, how what they just did will better inform them for future decision making.

WHAT IS ECONOMICS?

Economics is a **social science**. Biology, physics, and chemistry are natural sciences because they strive to unlock how the physical universe functions.

Social sciences such as psychology, sociology, and economics, on the other hand, study human behavior. This can be very challenging, as humans are not always consistent, either between two humans or even the same person two days in a row.

Consider two kids jumping off a high-dive at a swimming pool. They may do the exact same dive, but one did it because she loves the feeling of flying through the air, while the other did it reluctantly, fearfully, and only because he was dared to do it and didn't want to look like a "chicken" in front of his friends. It would be a huge problem to try and take into account every different motive of every person's actions every day, but fortunately many social scientists have discovered that, erratic as humans are, in large enough numbers we tend to be erratic in the same patterns. In economics, this might be seen in people spending too much for a shirt because its style or color is suddenly cool, though the quality of the shirt is otherwise unchanged.[3]

The study of such decision making, including both logical and illogical thinking, has come to be called **behavioral economics** and has been around since at least 1899 when Thorstein Veblen wrote *The Theory of the Leisure Class*, a book that looks into such things as why rich people who are otherwise good with money sometimes waste it by buying unnecessary and expensive things.

One might say behavioral economics came into its own in 2017 when Richard Thaler, one of the pioneers of modern behavioral economics and a key identifier of how consumers are "nudged" toward decisions, won the Nobel prize in economics. We will be using that term, **nudging**, mostly in the same sense he does, meaning that an otherwise conscious, rational decision about economic matters[4] (which for us, includes consumption of information as well as goods) is affected by other forces, including conscious nonrational factors, such as looking for coolness (chapter 5) and subconscious messaging by producers or speakers (chapter 9).

For all social sciences, a common method of investigation is by survey. Surveys allow for social scientists to collect lots of raw data and then look for a common pattern or some suggestion of a general rule. Many of the lessons in here are built on simple surveys[5] that students can conduct so that they can employ direct, student-centered investigation; move around in the "real world" as they consider the concepts; and most of all have fun. To the extent that these surveys are general and simplified for students, they are not the most airtight in variables but are rather designed more for students to get a taste of social science investigation. Still, students should observe some basic rules of conducting social science surveys:

- **Be safe!** Don't approach strangers unless adult-supervised and in a public place.

- **Be considerate.** If someone says they do not wish to participate, let them go. Try to take as little of their time as possible, and always thank them for their time at the end.
- **Be neutral.** You are not looking to prove your preconceived idea but to investigate the question by collecting data. Do not suggest an answer. Repeat the question if necessary or say, "I'm sorry, I'm not allowed to say more."
- **Be thorough.** Write down all the data you are supposed to collect at that time. Don't leave out anything because you don't like the response. Don't say, "I'll do it later," as you may forget, and be sure to write your information down so that another person can understand your information even if you aren't there to explain it.
- **Be a detective.** Data gathered doesn't actually give you any answers. You are like a detective; the conclusions come from your mind as you put all the pieces together. Once you have your data, look for patterns, rearrange things, and then write up what you think the data shows.
- **Have fun.** Surveying people is an adventure; you never know where it will lead. If you have an open mind, there is no limit to what you can find out. If you are enthusiastic, you will also find many more subjects will be so too, and you will get more data.

It would be a good idea to have your class write out these six "Be . . . " reminders on a large piece of butcher paper or a poster and post it somewhere in the classroom.

See **Lesson 2A—Socializing Science**

WHAT IS MEDIA LITERACY?

Literacy is generally thought of as the ability to read the printed word. As teachers know, however, fully understanding an author's message is much more than just decoding the literal language used. It's picking up nuance and implied messages and reading between the lines, and as we said before, most elementary kids are far from having a consistent working ability to do this, let alone with proficiency. A story may not explicitly say that two characters should be contrasted, but the author gives the reader every opportunity to do so (think of all the bad children in *Charlie and the Chocolate Factory* who are selfish and impetuous, compared to Charlie). Even pictures in a book help us to understand better what is going on. Imagine a young child telling a policeman there was "no problem," but then imagine all the different backgrounds that could change the meaning, from a nice day to a house on fire!

Literacy also means that a reader can better recognize when an author tries to make the audience feel a certain way, whether in regard to a fictional character (rooting for them to win) or in regard to a real-life issue (worried about the environment). The reader can then decide for herself whether to go along for the ride and enjoy the trip or be a bit removed so as not to be taken someplace emotionally she does not wish to go. Being truly literate in the reading sense, then, means not that someone has to read all the great books but, rather, that she is capable of reading any story and getting all she can from it.

Reading seems to be an art, a skill, or at least a pastime we are losing.[6] More people today are gravitating toward visual media or blended visual/verbal media rather than predominantly word-based media such as books.[7] Even so, the skills that were so important in purely reading still apply, perhaps more so today as the messages come to media consumers with greater ease and entertainment. The entertaining, fast-moving, and brightly colored video that someone watches on YouTube remains a message made by a particular person or group with a particular point of view that can affect the world perspective of those who consume it.

Added to this is the ubiquity of messaging, that there is virtually no place one can go without being bombarded not just by **information** but **persuasion**. **Media literacy**, then, is the ability to critically evaluate, understand, and decode messages to discern the difference between information and persuasion, to see what is both explicitly and implicitly messaged, and for the consumer of information ultimately to have more control of the diet of messaging they consume.

HOW DO ECONOMICS, BEHAVIORAL ECONOMICS, AND MEDIA LITERACY INTERACT?

Let's say a typical student sees an ad for a pair of cool shoes.[8] Classical economics (what most people think of) would study how the student weighs the price and quality of the shoes against other available shoes in making his decision whether to buy or not. **Behavioral economics** would study the intangible, even illogical, factors that go into the student's decision. Maybe he saw cool kids or a sports hero wearing the shoes, or he thinks back nostalgically to when he once won a championship wearing the same brand, or the color and style of the shoes are the same as a favorite "lucky" pair he had years ago.

Marketing would then try to convince the student to seal the deal and buy the shoes, perhaps by showing an admired athlete or cool pop star wearing them or how a kid who wears them is suddenly seen as cool by his peers. With all three of these areas, note that the student/potential buyer is on the passive, studied side of the discipline (even his decision making is innate or to a large extent subconscious).

With **media literacy**, the focus is turned around and our student-consumer takes the active role. How can the student recognize and break down all of the appeals being made to him to buy, and how can he decide which ones he wants to actually consider? How can the student be empowered with the tools necessary to be in more control of his own consumer decisions (such as resisting bullying by being called a loser for not following the herd), whether it be with tangible products like shoes or intangible ideas like political or social opinions?

Note that media literacy does not tell the student he should or should not consider a particular factor or even not consume something; rather, the goal is to leave such a decision up to the student, but with him as fully aware as possible of the nature and quality of the product or information proffered, the influences on him to consume, and the availability of alternative choices.

Behavioral economics and media lit go hand in glove, and to that end, to adequately educate students, one must cover the basic concepts of economics (chapter 3) and behavioral economics (chapter 4) to then see how media lit complements these disciplines and better empowers consumers of goods and media messaging in general. To put it another way, the art of conversation starts with listening and understanding the message being conveyed before one learns how to respond.

OH, WAIT! BEFORE WE BUCKLE UP AND START THE CAR, A NOTE ABOUT METHODOLOGY...

We will be suggesting throughout this book a number of recurring lesson formats. We should stress that all of these have been tested and found to work, but the teacher should feel free to modify as they see fit (and let us know!).[9]

For example, a number of the lessons ask students to watch TV shows and movies. Students can't analyze media unless they get a taste of it! Of course, kids love the idea of being assigned to watch TV, but it is important to review that they are *not* just kicking back and watching but actively viewing, recording, and analyzing what they see. It is left to the teacher's discretion in all cases whether the students can be assigned to do this on their own, with parental supervision, or as a group at school.

See **Lesson 2B—I Spy Science!**

Where possible, we have tried to make lessons into a game. Of course, each teacher must decide if and to what degree competition works within their class as a stimulant to learning or overshadows the beneficial qualities of the exercise. For our part, we have found that, while children do respond to an exercise in which "everyone can win," having some competitive measure, whether against another group or even against themselves (to better their time/score), adds an extra measure of interest and effort.

Another common lesson format is group discussion. There are so many ways this can be done, so we leave it to the teacher to decide, but four suggestions are proffered here:

1. **Circle talk:** informal discussion in small groups and few rules (to encourage open sharing), though many teachers use limits such as that no one may speak longer than one minute, everyone gets a turn, and there is an announced set time limit of discussion (five minutes). For elementary students, it works best if there is a requested end goal set ("Every person should share an example of an ad they saw and liked").
2. **Socratic seminar:** more structured than a circle talk, the students are given open-ended questions (such as the lessons in this book provide) that they must come to class prepared to discuss. They should bring notes or evidence, which contain both their thoughts and specific examples (such as from media) that support their ideas.

    The teacher (or assigned student discussion leader) throws out one of the open-ended questions as a "jump ball," such as "What should you do when you hear someone say, 'If you don't do this, you are a loser'?" The students then discuss (perhaps observing the rules of circle talk). If a question gets talked out, the group moves on to another question. If there are a large number of students, one group can sit on the outside of the circle, taking notes, switching places with the inner circle every five minutes or new question. After the Socratic circle is completed, students then write a post-discussion reflection (a sentence, paragraph, or short essay, depending on the level) in which they indicate what their position on the topic is.[10]
3. **Fishbowl:** This is a structured discussion that is designed to have maximum participation and keep a conversation evolving. Four chairs are placed in the center, two for each view. Only the people in the middle may speak. Any comments from outside can cause point deduction (if scored).[11] Once someone has spoken, they may be tagged out by someone on the same side of the issue. The tagger then takes the seat and remains until they have said something and are tagged out. The person tagged can finish their thought, however, before leaving.

    All comments made by a person are owned by that side. If Johnny says, "Martians are behind all advertising," and Susie tags in for him, she is stuck with the statement, as the idea is for a continuously moving but generally cohesive discussion. It also teaches cooperation even in a discussion format (like debate). If scoring, give 1 point for a strong point made, 2 points for a strong rebuttal, and 3 points if a person uses a real-world example as support. Everyone must observe the rules of respect, including addressing issues, not the people making them (**ad hominem fallacy**).

4. **Improv:** we also advocate using an improv format to add an element of fun. For those unfamiliar with it, students are divided into small groups (five is a good maximum)[12] in which they are given a general premise (buying something at a store), with certain specific elements (what they are buying) or an interrupting event (a tornado or the store forgot to pay its gravity utility bill) happening on the spot. Students must keep the action going and be creative in displaying and solving the problem. The new elements can be delivered either one or two minutes before performance (so that the group can plan) or put on an index card face down and turned over in the middle of the performance for immediate adaptation. Either way, the teacher should be equipped with multiple variables so no groups get the same ones (but get similar in kind). The main point is not to get it right but to keep the flow going and have fun. This format has been well-received at all levels of students; even naysayers usually get into it as the rest of the class has fun with it (but we'll explore peer pressure later!).

CHAPTER 2 ACCOMPANYING LESSONS

Lesson 2A — Socializing Science

Key Concepts
   Economics as a social science, studying aggregated human behavior
Special Materials/Media
   Computer to run spreadsheet program (optional if the teacher wishes to tie the lesson with spreadsheet usage)
Intro Questions/Thoughts for Students

- If you take a large number of individual things (like trees), can you make assumptions about them when you look at large groups of them?
- You are all individuals, with your own likes and dislikes, but do you think there are any patterns with groups of people (like everyone likes sweets)?
- Can assumptions about groups of people be useful? When are they helpful and when are they not?

Activity

Introduce students to the scientific method in the following manner:

1. Ask students generally as a class if they think the members of the class are more similar or different. Then pose the two following specific questions: *What is something that can be said about everyone in the class as a whole? What is something that can be said about most members of the class?* Explain to students that asking such initial questions is the first step to scientific inquiry and discovery, from Sir Francis Bacon to studying the edges of our universe today.
2. Students should now talk in small groups, each taking turns talking for roughly one minute about himself or herself, including information about where they were born, favorite things, travels, or hobbies. Explain that the information they are generally gathering is part of the second step of experiments called research.
3. From this research, each student should now formulate a hypothesis, an educated guess or preliminary answer to the questions posed above.
4. Now it's time to experiment. In physical sciences this usually means setting up a lab, but in social sciences, it often means conducting a survey to see responses (and sometimes altering the survey in different ways to see if the results vary). In this case, have students develop a survey that asks general questions, such as:

   - What are your favorite and least favorite foods?
   - How many countries have you visited?
   - Where were you born?
   - Who is your favorite music artist?

   Have everyone in the class fill it out. If possible, have students from other classes/grades also fill out the survey.
5. Now comes the analysis and drawing conclusions. Have the students then tally results and try to formulate general statements, such as "We like superhero movies." They can also make bar graphs or pie charts to illustrate the general trends of "Who we are."

Follow-up Questions/Discussions

- Were you surprised by any "winners" in each category?
- Were any of your hypotheses way off?
- Were some trends by a lot or by a little?

- How could a person studying or doing a report on the class use this information? What about a marketer (someone trying to sell a product to the class)?
- What might be a problem of assuming all members of a group act or think in agreement with a majority of that group?
- Follow-up lesson: A good researcher always takes a moment to not only analyze the data but look back and see if the methodology (way the experiment was run) might have an effect on the results or could be improved. Discuss some ways you could repeat the experiment but make it better:

  - Ask more people (bigger sample size).
  - Reword the question.
  - Change the order of the questions.
  - Change whether the survey is given as a group (where people might call out or look at others' responses) or done in private.

Social Questions for Students

- If one of your responses (such as favorite movie) was the most common, how did that make you feel? What if your favorite was the least liked by others?

Lesson 2B—I Spy Science!

Key Concepts
   Careful observations as key to scientific inquiry
Special Materials/Media
   Tally sheet (see figure 2.1)
Intro Questions/Thoughts for Students

- How do scientists "discover" or learn about things? How do they find answers to questions they have about the world?
- How is being a scientist like being a detective? What are the "clues" scientists look for and how do they find them?
- Which of your senses do you use the most to find out things about the world?

Activity

A fun way to introduce the power of careful observation is to use the public service announcement titled *Test Your Awareness: Do The Test* found at https://www.youtube.com/watch?v=Ahg6qcgoay4. You may have to play it several times to convince the students the gorilla was there!

Ask the students why they didn't see the gorilla. Was it because they weren't expecting it? How important is it, then, to be open to seeing new things, not only for safety (like the video promotes) but in order to learn new things?

Now hand out a tally sheet like below, which students will use on the playground (such as at recess).

Each student (or in teams) should try to find three things for each category. Afterward, the students put together a large class list.

Follow-up Questions/Discussions

- Were some categories easier to find things for than others? Why do you think that is?
- Were some of the things you found ordinary (everyday) and other things special (unusual)? Which did you have more of?
- Why do you think it is important to put down where you were? Did students who were far away from each other see similar or different things?
- Scientists like it when other scientists do the same things they do, like repeat an experiment/observation. The more they do that, the more things they can discover together. Did you find that to be true?

Social Questions for Students

- We sometimes get so used to something, or someone, we stop looking for new things about them. See if you can find something new and fun about a place or person you already know by observing them.
- What do you think people could learn or think about you if they watched you for a day? What would you want them to learn or think about you?

Name: _____

Where was I sitting? _____

Things I saw:

About people	1.
	2
	3.
About the place	1.
	2
	3.
About what was going on (action)	1.
	2
	3.

Figure 2.1. Tally sheet

NOTES

1. Teachers know most kids don't even have the patience to let you get in the classroom door before telling you about their dog eating cheese and throwing it up last night, let alone waiting for you to put on your lifesaving oxygen mask first.

2. See http://www.ashidakim.com/zenkoans/1acupoftea.html. Pardon the yen for Zen, here, but people tend to come into a discussion of economics expecting confusing numbers and boring, long-winded explanations. We hope to dispel these notions (at least the confusing

numbers part) before we take off on the exciting world we have come to love—and believe you will, too.

3. This following-the-herd effect, even counter to good sense, can be seen in finance with bubbles and in communication with people going along with messages they don't agree with. In fact, the impulse to collective decision making is factored into things such as designing emergency exiting on planes: https://corescholar.libraries.wright.edu/cgi/viewcontent.cgi?article=1035&context=isap_2017. See also Lesson 5D on the **bandwagon effect**.

4. Richard Thaler and Cass Sunstein, *Nudge: Improving Decisions about Health, Wealth and Happiness* (New York: Penguin Books, 2009), 8.

5. Depending on the level of elementary students, we recommend the students predesign the survey and then have the teacher (after gently smoothing out the questions) print the sheet out so students can just read them off to test subjects and then mark predesignated columns for responses.

6. See Caleb Crain, "Why We Don't Read, Revisited," *The New Yorker*, June 14, 2018, https://www.newyorker.com/culture/cultural-comment/why-we-dont-read-revisited.

7. See Michelle Krasniak, "Visual Content and Social Media Marketing: New Research," *Social Media Examiner*, May 30, 2017, https://www.socialmediaexaminer.com/visual-content-and-social-media-marketing-new-research/, or Victoria Malabrigo, "Visual Content on Social Media: 2017 Trends and Research," WNET/New York Public Media Interactive Engagement Group, March 13, 2017, https://ieg.wnet.org/2017/03/visual-content-social-media-2017-trends-research/.

8. Again, we repeat that this is not for the kids to understand the nuanced differences explained here. This is for the teacher's understanding so that she can then be adept at helping guide the student.

9. We are also cognizant that most of our lessons assume at least limited access to the Internet, and while in this day and age, this should be unquestionably available for all students, it is unfortunately not so.

10. A nice add-on is for the teacher to supply slips of paper that say "I really like what _____ said about _____ because _____" for the students to practice listening and to help kids feel good about participating.

11. This is also a great lesson on patience and waiting one's turn!

12. As improv is an intense but short-term cooperative challenge, a randomizer program of names, such as https://www.random.org/lists/, keeps groups new each time the exercises are done. On the other hand, teachers may find the exercise valuable to put particular students together to "nudge" them to appreciate and cooperate with each other. We won't tell!

Chapter Three

Introduction to Basic Economics

The Objective Study of Choice

HOW TO INTRODUCE ECONOMICS TO THE CLASS

Most every teacher is familiar with "Would you rather . . . ?" questions for students, but here are two[1]:

- If everything cost $1, but you only had $1 right now, would you rather buy fruit, chips, or a drink?
- If the next class was a free period, would you rather have a study hall, play outside, or sit and talk with other students?

There are many variations of these questions,[2] but you get the idea.

Each time you offer a choice, ask a student in each group to say *why* they chose that option. If possible, try to get the student to say more than "Because I like it the most." Then, after doing this exercise a couple of times, ask the students what they noticed about the choices they made and what happened:

- What choices were the most popular? Why do you think that is?
- Were there any patterns as to who chose what?
- What might they do with the information they have figured out about the choices, patterns, and trends? If they opened a store in the school, what would they sell based on the survey? If they were a teacher, what would they plan for the students to do on the next free day?

And now, the punchline: Congratulate the students for becoming **economists**!

Economics is the study of choice and, in particular, how we choose to spend **resources**. Resources are what goes into making something. In the first example above, the resource was $1, but there was only enough to choose one item. Which one was the best thing to spend money on? In the second example, the class was given one free period, not three, so they had to choose the best way to spend their time (which is a resource, too, because it allows you to make and do things).

Think of a pencil. There's the wood and graphite that the pencil is made of, but there also needs to be a machine that put it all together and people who run the machines. All these are resources that helped make a pencil.

Generally, we like to say there are three kinds of resources, called the **factors of production**[3]:

1. Land—the raw materials used to make the good.
2. Labor—the persons who put in effort to make the good and bring it to sale.
3. Capital—the machines and tools used to make the good.

Even something simple, like a fast-food burger, can have lots of resources that went into making it. Land factors include the meat, lettuce, grains, even down to the tomatoes that became ketchup. For labor, the obvious person one thinks of is the guy at the counter who sold it to you, but if you think of the long line behind him, it includes the cook, the person who delivered the food to the store, the warehouse people, continuing back to the farmer or rancher!

As for capital, there are all the machines and systems that went into bringing that meal to you, from the cash register back to the fryers to the trucks and tractors. It almost boggles the mind to think of yourself sitting in the middle of a circle composed of all the people and things that went into your one moment, so you better appreciate it and eat it all! Money falls into the capital factor, as it is a tool for the producer in order to acquire the land, labor, and machines that then make the burger.

As we said before, the "Would you rather . . . ?" choices involved using money and time, so what kind of resources are those? They aren't raw materials, so they are not land, nor are they people, so they are not labor. They are, however, tools that help us get what we want and get things done, so they are capital!

See **Lesson 3A — Voice Your Choice**

See **Lesson 3B — Be Resourceful**

See **Lesson 3C — Contents Contest**

WHY DO WE NEED ECONOMICS?

There is no government agency devoted to preserving gravity because, though we find it really helpful, we aren't afraid of gravity running out anytime soon. On the other hand, when people became concerned we might use up or pollute clean air and water, Congress created the Environmental Protection Agency (EPA) in 1970 to help give advice and regulate the use of natural resources, so that we can make the best choices about how to use and preserve them.

So, when the EPA was formed, they of course hired lots of scientists to get **data** about the environment and what was going on, but they also hired a bunch of—you guessed it—economists to talk about what might be the best choices to make in using air and water. If economics studies our choices, it can then be used to help us make the best decisions for ourselves and our community in using **scarce goods**. These are things of which there are few but that are in demand. That's a little different than things that are **rare**, which there are few of them but that they may or may not be wanted. Both diamonds and five-legged cats are rare, but since most people only want diamonds out of the two, the diamonds are also scarce.

See **Lesson 3D — No! Mine!**

How few of something does there have to be for something to be considered scarce? There is no set number; it's really just about there being fewer of the things desired than there are people who want them. In the 1990s, there were thousands of Beanie Babies produced, but because more people wanted them than there were the actual toys, they were scarce (and scary when adults got into shoving matches in toy stores over them!). So, when your students are deciding if they'll watch a TV show or play a computer game, they are engaging in an economic decision regarding using the scariest resource of all: time (because you can never make more!).

Economics, then, helps us to decide how best to use scarce resources. It also helps others to know how to use resources for the good of all. In the "Would you rather . . . ?" exercise, some choices had a clear favorite, while others were close. Looking at these choice patterns (which is what economists do), they can recommend choices to be offered to people making the choices on the using/buying end (called consumers). Put it another way, if you said "Peanut butter and . . . ," many would say jelly, but some might say bananas or just want their peanut butter "straight up." Few would say "Brussels sprouts." This kind of information would be helpful to a restaurant in making a children's menu as to what to offer (perhaps saving the restaurant owners from sitting sadly on a huge bag of Brussels sprouts they bought).

MONEY FOR NOTHIN' . . .

For all the choices all over the world that economics and economists are involved with, people most often think about economics as it relates to making decisions about money. It is true that it is a big, maybe even the biggest, part of economic decision making, but it is important to remember that money is not the end goal for either *producers* or *consumers* of things (or, as will be often referred to here, sellers and buyers). Money itself is nothing more than a tool; it is a means to an end, with the end usually being for both sellers and buyers to acquire things that they perceive will make their lives better and more enjoyable, from food and shelter to vacations and luxury items.

Money is important because it's a helpful tool for getting things as a **medium of exchange**, meaning it's an agreed-upon representation of a product's value. Before money, people traded goods for other goods (**barter system**), but this had severe limits.

For one, both parties had to want each other's goods for trade to happen. To help students understand, ask them to rate how much they like apples. One student may love apples and would give away ten of her pencils for one red delicious; another may not like them as much so only might give away one or two pencils, or none at all. We thus can't be sure as a group what an apple is worth, but with money, we can all understand what one dollar represents.

Money, whether metal coin or paper bill, also has at least two other advantages. First, it's easy to carry around (think of a rancher having to pull a steer out of his pocket to pay for a meal at a restaurant!); and second, it keeps its value, meaning it doesn't turn bad very quickly like a bushel of bananas would. A wrinkled, dirty dollar is worth the same as a crisp, new one.

See **Lesson 3E—Money for Nothin'**

CHOOSING—THE TRADE-OFF

So, you are a student with a lot of homework (or a teacher with lots of grading), but you also want to see the latest episode of that TV show you love. How do you (and, generally, all consumers) make the choice? First, let's recognize the scarce resource in this scenario: *time*. You don't have time to do both in one evening, so you'll need to *spend* your time on either the schoolwork or the TV show.

When someone has to choose between one thing (choice A) and another (choice B) that is called a **trade-off**. Most people hate trade-offs because you can't get both things that you want, but this is where the economist becomes a superhero and bursts in with her mighty tool, a **cost-benefit analysis**.[4]

Most people have heard of this kind of analysis, but when they do it, they only do it halfway. Take the student in the example above. He might write down a list of benefits to each choice, labeling each good thing as +1 if he likes it and +2 if he likes it a lot[5] (table 3.1).

As choice B is a 6 but the schoolwork is a 5, it would seem the show wins. However, this is only half the job; it's only a benefit-benefit trade-off. To do a real **cost-benefit analysis**, the student would list the costs of doing each (the bad things that could happen) and mark them as -1 (bad) and -2 (really bad) (table 3.2).

Now, one more part to the magic trick. Each choice has to have its costs subtracted from its benefits (table 3.3).

Lo and behold, factoring in the potential negative consequences means that choosing to study has a higher value than watching TV, so it probably is the better choice (did you really expect different in an educational manual?). This may look complicated, but it is actually what we all do in our head if we thoroughly consider options when making a choice. We may not list out pros and cons or assign formal numbers, but even an impressionistic, quick decision is made this way, even if at a gut level, and the beauty of this kind of analysis is that it works for just about every choice!

The other important lesson for this process is that, in weighing two choices (or even deciding whether to do or not do one action), what we are actually weighing are the *consequences* or results of our choices. All choices have consequences, and to the extent we know them in advance, we take responsibility for those consequences.

Table 3.1.

Benefits of Choice A		Benefits of Choice B	
Schoolwork		*TV show*	
better chance for good grade	+1	entertainment	+2
parents happy	+2	can talk about show with friends	+2
helps me for next lesson	+2	helps me to be "cool"	+2
Total Benefit Score	**5**		**6**

Table 3.2.

Costs of Choice A		Costs of Choice B	
Not watching TV show		*Not studying*	
miss out on show for one night	-1	parents disappointed	-2
may have spoiler given away by friend	-2	parents take away TV	-2
may give up another show to catch up	-1	behind other students	-1
		will have to give up a weekend night to study	-2
Total Cost Score	**-4**		**-7**

Table 3.3.

Choosing A (Schoolwork)		Choosing B (TV show)	
Benefits of A	5	Benefits of B	6
Costs of A	-4	Costs of B	-7
Benefit score	**1**		**-1**

See **Lesson 3F—Trade-Offs Are On!**

CHANGING OUR MINDS (AND CHOICE)

The choices are ours, but that doesn't mean we always know why we are making those choices. We'll discuss how outside forces (like ads) influence our choices, but for now let's look a little closer at the most frequently given reason why someone says they chose something: because they "liked" it. What does that mean? There are a lot of things that go into liking something, but there are a couple of things going on inside the chooser that helps them say, "I want this, not that."

The first internal influencer is how useful for us we think one thing will be over another. This is called its **utility**. A car is more useful than a snack, but until you are old enough to drive one, maybe enjoy the snack! There are also things that get less useful after a while, like a cotton swab or a tennis ball. They can get pretty used up (and icky) fast, so it's better to switch to a new one or switch to a different activity in the case of tennis. This is called a product's **marginal utility**, or the benefit we get from consuming (using) one additional product.

After school a girl stops by a convenience store with two dollars in her pocket. She is thirsty and hungry, but her thirst (on our always handy 1–10 scale) is an 8 and her hunger is a 6. Given she can buy either one drink or one snack, she will opt for the drink because it has a higher marginal utility. It will, relative to price, satisfy her more.

Let's say that after she drinks, she finds two more dollars in her other pocket. She weighs her choices again, but now finds that whereas her hunger is still a 6, her thirst has dropped to a 5.[6] This is because of the law of diminishing return that for the same amount of resources put in (here, two dollars), one gets less benefit. It's a fancy way of saying things get old and explains why even the best toy can get boring after a while or that one can only study so much. Back to our girl in the convenience store, because of the new comparative marginal utilities, she will switch her choice and purchase the snack, as it has the higher marginal utility now (6 compared to 5). In a nutshell, this is why people change their minds!

See **Lesson 3G — No More, Please!**

For many years, economics only studied the "brain" part of making choices, but what about when the "heart" makes its emotional preferences known? Sure, we want to know how much something costs (price) and how good it is (quality), but what about other things, like what using such a product says about who I am?

Look at just about any ad and you'll find a lot more being said about a product than its price and quality. Some of the ads seem irrational, if not downright fantastical. Either all these advertisers are off the mark, or they know that there are other factors that consumers consider, maybe even ones consumers (especially children) are not consciously aware of, making them vulnerable to advertisers sneaking into their cost-benefit analysis, like a thief through an unlocked back door. What are those nonrational appeals, and even more, how can children learn how to check and lock that back door to unwanted intrusion? Welcome to behavioral economics and media literacy!

See **Lesson 3H — Write the Powers That Be!**

CHAPTER 3 ACCOMPANYING LESSONS

Lesson 3A — Voice Your Choice

Key Concepts
　　Economics as the study of choices/decision making, **scarcity**
Special Materials/Media
　　A log sheet (see table 3.4)
Intro Questions/Thoughts for Students

- How often do you have to make choices in a day? Is there a pattern to your decision making?
- Is there a general rule you have in deciding between two choices?

Activity

Students keep a log for a day. Every time they are faced with a choice and decision, they should fill out a log (expand as necessary) as follows:

Table 3.4.

Choice A	Choice B	Why couldn't I have both?	Which did I choose?	Why?

Follow-up Questions/Discussions

- Do you see a pattern in the kinds of choices you have to make?
- Is there a recurring reason why you had to make a choice (lack of time, money)?
- Is there a pattern to why you chose things? Does it fit the "general rule" you said before the activity (which became a hypothesis)?[7]

Social Questions for Students

- When would you rather not be given a choice?

Lesson 3B—Be Resourceful

Key Concepts
   Factors of production
Special Materials/Media
   None
Intro Questions/Thoughts for Students

- We think of something, like a pencil, as a thing, but it is made of a lot of other things (wood, graphite, paint). It also required people who made it and tools and machines to cut the parts and fit them all together. These are called the factors of production. Almost everything is made up of something else.

Activity

Part 1—The teacher explains the three types of factors of production (land, labor, and capital), drawing the three categories on the board. She then calls out everyday classroom items (paper, adhesive tape, the chairs) and helps students to see the factors of production that made them.

Part 2—The teacher has students find something at home and come to next class explaining the object and some of the factors of production for that object.

Part 3—Students use a variety of supplies (paper, pipe cleaners, paper clips, etc.) to create an invention that they think would make the world better or more fun. They then present their invention and what it does but also explain the factors of production that made it.

Follow-up Questions/Discussions

- Were some factors harder to figure out than others?
- Were some factors always the same (people to put it together)?
- Is labor just the people who put the object like a pencil together? What about the people who grow the trees or even the person who invented the pencil?
- Is the time it takes to work on something a factor? How so?
- We seem to have a lot of people to make things, but can we run out of things (like trees) to make things out of? Why is it important to reduce, reuse, and recycle resources?

Social Questions for Students

- What about making yourself good at something, like a good student, dancer, or athlete? What are the factors that go into making that?
- A lot of people have put their time, hard work, and love into making you the best person you can be. They are factors of your production! Unlike a pencil, however, you can appreciate and thank them. Write a thank-you note to someone who has been a factor in making *you*.

Lesson 3C—Contents Contest

Key Concepts
    Factors of production
Special Materials/Media
    Index cards for the teacher
Intro Questions/Thoughts for Students

- When you use something, do you ever stop and think about how many resources went into it or how many people worked to bring you that moment of enjoyment?

Activity

Divide the class into three teams. Have two sets of index cards, one set that identifies the categories of factors of production ("land," "labor," and "capital") and another with a wide variety of products and activities, such as a hamburger, a pencil, a textbook, electricity for one's home, or a professional sporting event.

The teacher randomly calls out one of the product groups and calls out a category for factors of production, either "land," "labor," or "capital."

The groups then have three to five minutes to make a list of people or things that fall into that category in regard to that product or activity.

At the end of the time, groups take turns calling out one item on their list. They get one point for every item they say that is on only one other team's list and two points if it is on no one else's list (adjust depending on how many groups there are). The teacher is the judge as to whether an item is directly associated enough to count.

Follow-up Questions/Discussions

- How far back in the creation of the product or activity did you have to go to get something unique? What is the farthest back anyone went?
- Did you include people or things that improved the product? (Basketball was originally played with literal baskets, but then someone came up with the idea of a metal hoop and netting.)

Social Questions for Students

- Whom are you a factor in production for? Whom do you help make their lives better? What can you do to help others?
- Besides your teachers, who are all the other people that help make your school function? What can you do to thank them and show appreciation for what they do?

Lesson 3D—No! Mine!

Key Concepts
   Scarcity versus **rarity**, scarcity as affected by demand
Special Materials/Media
   Index cards

Intro Questions/Thoughts for Students

- Have you ever seen something and immediately wanted it? Why did you go so quickly from not knowing it existed to wanting it?
- Have you ever wanted something because someone else had it? Why do you think that made you want it?

Activity

The teacher brings in several items of the same quality but different styles (equal value and utility), such as different Hot Wheels cars, small stuffed animals, or marker sets, and hands them out to each student. The kids get to play with or use theirs for two to three minutes. Then they can look for one minute at what the others have and decide if they want to trade. Take turns trading, much like a white elephant gift exchange. If they want someone else's, they can trade theirs for the other. They can, of course, decide to keep their own unless someone else wants theirs. After the trades have all taken place, give the students two to three more minutes to play with their new items.

Follow-up Questions/Discussions

- Did you trade yours for someone else's? Why?
- Who kept theirs? Why?
- How did it feel to lose yours?
- After playing with yours, was there an allure to the others?
- If they are all of equal value and utility, why trade at all? Is the grass always greener?
- Have you ever really wanted something, but once you got it, it wasn't as enjoyable or fun as you thought it would be? Maybe everyone should make a list of those kinds of things as well. What does that tell you about wanting versus having?

Social Questions for Students

- When you are jealous that someone has something you don't have, what can you do so you don't feel so jealous?
- Things and experiences look fun for others, but how can we know if it is right (or going to be fun) for us? Is it OK to not like something everyone else likes?

Lesson 3E — Money for Nothin'

Key Concepts
   Currency, money as a created system for exchange of value
Special Materials/Media
   Quantities of different items found in a classroom or home, such as paper clips, pencils, pieces of paper or tape, sticky notes, etc.
Intro Questions/Thoughts for Students

- What is money?
- Why do we use it?
- What makes money valuable?

Activity

Your students' school (or house) is now its own country. It will take a while to get things up and running, but in the meantime, they will need some sort of money (**currency**) to buy and sell goods (food, pencils, etc.) for their country. Have students look around and decide what is best to use for money.
   Some questions students should consider in designating something as money:

- Does it "store value" (doesn't rot, like a banana would)?
- Is it easy to recognize and can people agree on its value (does a long pencil = a short one?)?
- Is it easy to carry around?
- Can you make change with it?

Have students compare their choices. What are the advantages and disadvantages of each choice?

Follow-up Questions/Discussions

- Did most people choose something as money that also had a practical use (e.g., a pencil) or something only useful as money (pieces of paper)? What are the advantages and disadvantages of each?
- Why do you think cultures moved from trading things (barter) to using money?
- What happens if you choose as currency something that there are too many of (paper clips)? What happens to the price of things (**inflation**)?

Social Questions for Students

- Did you choose something as money that was good for yourself (such as something you have a lot of) or good for most people in your classroom/country (something everyone has)? How do you decide which to go with if you can't find something that does both? What happens if everyone chooses just what's best for them?

Lesson 3F—Trade-Offs Are On!

Key Concepts
   Cost-benefit trade-off decision-making process
Special Materials/Media
   None
Intro Questions/Thoughts for Students

- How do you make decisions? Do you have a method or do you go with your gut?

Activity

Have each student think of an either/or choice they need to make. It can be studying versus video games, whether or not to go to a party, or choosing between two kinds of food. For both options, the students should write out the benefits of choosing each as well as the costs or negatives.

Students then assign numbers as explained in table 3.5 (+1 or +2 for good/really good benefits, -1 or -2 for really bad costs) and then total and compare the numbers. The number should just be a gut feeling or reaction; no need to heavily weigh it out or consider just the right number. The choice with the higher total is the winner!

Table 3.5.

Choice A	Choice B
Benefits (what gained) of choosing A (+1 for each good benefit, +2 for each really good benefit)	Benefits (what gained) of choosing B (+1 for each good benefit, +2 for each really good benefit)
Costs (consequences) of choosing A (-1 for each bad cost, -2 for each really bad cost)	Costs (consequences) of choosing B (-1 for each bad cost, -2 for each really bad cost)
Total for Choice A (benefits − costs)	**Total for Choice B (benefits − costs)**

Follow-up Questions/Discussions

- Does the choice that "won" using the method above agree with what you thought "in your gut" would win beforehand? If it didn't work, why do you think it did not?

Social Questions for Students

- When is it better to put a lot of thought into making a choice? Try using this system for that kind of decision.

Lesson 3G—No More, Please!

Key Concepts
  Law of diminishing return, **marginal utility**
Special Materials/Media
  Sweet soft drink, cookies, candy, or other desired treats
Intro Questions/Thoughts for Students

- Why and when do consumers choose or change what they consume?

Activity

Test subjects (*consumers*) are asked to rate on a scale of 1–10 how much they want a cookie and how much they want a drink. Whichever one they want more, they are given. After a moment, they are asked again to rate how much they want to consume an additional unit of both items and to consume whichever they rank higher. The test is conducted at least until they switch the product consumed.
  Testers make a chart/graph of the numbers (perhaps in conjunction with a math class).

Follow-up Questions/Discussion

- Why did the consumer switch to another product? Why did the score of wanting one more of the thing (called marginal utility) go down?
- What else can you think of that loses marginal utility (stops being fun)? Do even fun activities (playing a game, attending a party) get boring after a while? Do they happen at different speeds (rates), with some things being more fun or satisfying longer than others?

Social Questions for Students

- Do you ever get tired of being with someone, even someone you like? Is that OK? What can you do or say when this happens? How would you react if a friend told you they needed a break from you for a little bit?

Lesson 3H — Write the Powers That Be!

Key Concepts
   Empowerment of consumers
Special Materials/Media
   Computer to research companies and to send e-mail
Intro Questions/Thoughts for Students

- Have you ever had a toy or used a product and thought, "This would make it better"?
- How about the way something is given out (like a cafeteria line)? Can that be made better? Or how you can enjoy the product or thing with less waste (such as using less packaging)?
- Do you think companies like to hear how their products and services can be made better?

Activity

1. Students should think of something they consume for which they can think of some way to improve it:

   - Can the product be improved (more flavors, change how it works)?
   - Did the use of the product meet their expectations (the parts wore out too fast)?
   - Can the way it is given out (in the store, packaging) be made better?
   - How about the store that sells it (layout, cleanliness, helpfulness of staff)?

2. Students should look up the company that made or sold the product (depending on the nature of their suggestion) and find the contact information online (usually under a tab or section labeled "contact us"). Students should then write a letter expressing their opinion as to how the product/sales can be improved.
3. Before sending the letter, students should practice proofreading both their own letter and at least one other person's to make sure the meaning is clear and that the tone is proper. It also doesn't hurt to have parents review and OK the letter.

4. Students should send off the letters and then wait to see if they receive a reply. (NOTE: A return e-mail address is usually asked for. Students should get parental permission to offer theirs, or the teacher can use his/hers or create a class one.)
5. As a second follow-up, students should repeat the activity above but find a product and send a *complimentary* e-mail in praise of the product or buying experience.

Follow-up Questions/Discussions

- Were the responses that you received more automatic/form responses or personalized? Which do you like better?
- Any surprise responses? If the class can, have a contest for "best response by a company" and perhaps let them know.
- Why is it important to also send compliments to companies? Why do you think people are often more likely to send complaints rather than compliments?
- Why is it important to be firm but not rude in expressing oneself?
- Did you proofread thoroughly, or did you find mistakes after you sent it? What do you think happens to the strength of your opinion if it is expressed poorly, such as with spelling errors?

Social Questions for Students

- Have you ever had to make a helpful suggestion to a friend because you did not like the way they did something? Was it hard? Why?
- Do you think it's important to give compliments once in a while to your friends? Why? Can you "overdo it"?

NOTES

1. Choice exercise are often a good place to get students up and moving, such as putting them in the middle of the class and, as you call out the choices, point to corners of the room they have to go to demonstrate their choices. Not only is this more active for the kids, but it teaches ancillary lessons like listening to *all* the choices, following directions, and seeing with whom they share preferences. You can also address those students who habitually have difficulty committing or making a choice.

2. See, for example, https://conversationstartersworld.com/would-you-rather-questions-for-kids/.

3. A fourth factor, *entrepreneurship*, is sometimes added, but for simplicity's sake, we'll keep it out for now. For more precise economic terminology, we humbly point you in the direction of *Middle Schoolers: Meet Media Literacy* and its more mature companion, *High Schoolers: Meet Media Literacy*, available at finer Internet sites.

4. The following explanation is a very simplified version of a cost-benefit analysis. Of course, the ideas and process for doing such an analysis are built upon this foundation in the other books. See note 3.

5. We sometimes use a 1–3 scale so there is more variation in numbers.
6. It helps students to draw on the board a "hunger scale" and a "thirst scale" with numbers from 10 down to 1 vertically.
7. See Lesson 2A.

Chapter Four

Behavioral Economics

How We Are "Nudged" While Making Our Choices

Let's talk about funerals. We begin the chapter this way for two reasons. First, we want to lay claim to being the first—and possibly only—teacher manual/lesson book to begin a chapter with that sentence. Second, funerals are a great example of the forces of what's called **behavioral economics** at work.

Considering the matter at hand in regard to a funeral, costs for items such as a casket should be low. Most of such items purchased are a one-time use, and the ultimate user, you should pardon, is not in a position or condition to complain. Yet, the average price of a casket is about $2,000 according to the Federal Trade Commission, with some "high-end" ones selling for $10,000! The overall average price of a funeral and burial according to the FTC is between $7,000 and $10,000.

So why do we spend so much? It's hard to justify such costs by the rational factors of price and quality explained in the last chapter, so we'll have to add new ones, specifically nonrational, emotional motivators such as love, gratitude, and sometimes even guilt. In this case, "**nonrational factors**" is preferable to "irrational factors" as "nonrational" conveys that such factors are *in addition to* the rational ones, rather than negative ones in opposition to rational factors. After all, wanting to spend a lot to show appreciation for a beloved person's final rest appeals to many, if not most, people, and it is exactly that kind of common sentiment that makes so many people responsive to ads that say they will help you in a time of grief or even that one should pre-purchase a plan to save one's children the stress.

All of this talk of funerals (which, we remind you, begins with "fun") is to get a grasp of behavioral economics, which takes the traditional economics described in the last chapter and broadens the study to include social and psychological factors that influence our economic choices.

The most popular examples of behavioral economics are the *Freakonomics* books by Steven Levitt. Levitt and his associates show that psychological factors can not only reinforce but even counter rational factors, such as when Israeli day-care facilities added a small monetary penalty for parents who picked up their children late. Rather than the added financial punishment acting as a disincentive, decreasing the number of late parents, the charge *increased* the number of late parents as it removed the greater guilt disincentive on the other side of the cost-benefit scales that made some parents rush to pick up their children on time. Such emotional factors become nudges toward a certain choice, whether in the realm of economics or in information selection (such as whom to believe). These nudges can be subtle, subliminal, and perhaps even insidious.

We are more likely to believe our friend's version of how a car accident happened rather than a stranger's (unless we know our friend is a bad driver), and we will subconsciously demand more proof from the stranger to be swayed to his version of events. Worst of all, such tacit factors may be known and even utilized by those trying to nudge us in a direction, and unless consumers are aware of such influences by way of media literacy, we will fall prey to it and make choices that are not in our own best interest or perhaps even harmful.

CHILDREN AND "NUDGING"

Whatever is true about people in general being susceptible to emotional nudging is especially true in children. Their powers of rational problem solving have not yet developed, and they are looking for clues and guides as to what is the "right" choice.

There is not a parent who hasn't nudged their child even while giving the illusion of independent decision making. One of our own children once came in from playing totally covered in dirt, to which the crafty, duplicitous parent said, "It's totally up to you; you can take a bath in the downstairs tub or the upstairs one." The child gleefully celebrated their empowerment and ability to call the shots.[1]

Elementary teachers well know this, and experienced ones apply the nudge with deft skills. "Learning this will help prepare you for fourth grade." "I like the way Sherice got out her pencil and paper without having to be told to do so." There's even the anti-nudge, such as "I'm afraid if we don't settle down and get things done, we won't have time for a story at the end."

As we will also explore later, children have an extra driver in their thinking that makes them actually want to be nudged. Whereas with teenagers, a direct "older people do this" might elicit a rejection of the proffered action, children will embrace it like a "This Way" sign. This is called **aspirational buying** or the consumption of products in order to imitate a group one wants to belong to, in the case of children, being older. If you have ever been to a foreign country, where you intentionally hesitate a second so you can see what the locals do and then imitate them so as to blend in as best you can (or at least not offend), you know what a child is going through with aspirational thinking and buying. No matter how good a swimmer we are, we all can't resist huge waves that push us along.[2]

See **Lesson 4A — Is That Us?**

Aspirational buying isn't just for tangible products, either. We want to believe in those we trust and look to for guidance, and part of that is taking their opinion as the right one. Consider children's views of politicians and political parties: How many of the children who say, "I like her/him for president," are basing it on measured study of the issues, and how many are basing it on what they hear at the dinner table?

THE ART OF THE NUDGE

The first step in studying "under the radar"[3] nudging is to realize how much of it we take for granted. We are bombarded with logos, ads, and persuasive messages that may not register consciously. Right now, look up and around; how long did it take you to see a logo or brand name? One well-placed brand name or logo will not cause a complete shift in opinion, but in total such messaging might form our opinions and tastes over time, like the formation of huge cave stalagmites from tiny drops of calcified water over centuries. That is why we liken cumulative advertising to the formation of a stalagmite in a cave: drop by drop, almost imperceptibly it grows until one day you bang into it. This is especially true for children, where time to build a stalagmite of the child's preferences is on the marketer's side.

See **Lesson 4B — Count on It**

Added to this general effect is that, even while we are aware that we are looking for something definitive that we need (such as food when we are hungry), we may not be self-aware of what we are also emotionally seeking. People are sometimes asked to do a "gut check" of what they believe or want, but often this is less a request that they should listen to their "gut" so much as become self-aware of the message *they have been listening to already*, like suddenly being quiet and realizing the sounds that have been there the whole time.

When we make choices, it often feels like we are making a decision in that isolated moment, sometimes even saying, "I just want this right now." What we don't see is all of the things that brought us to that moment, including where we see ourselves in the big picture. Even children bring a lifetime of experiences that they may not remember, such as that teacher who gave out chocolate candy kisses for correct answers or an admired family member who always drove one kind of car. Every one of these quick interactions with a particular seller of a product is called a **brand impression**, and as noted before, they can add up, like the cheer of individual people can combine into a deafening stadium roar.

We also bring the way we currently see ourselves and let those self-perceptions guide us in choosing. If a girl sees herself as an athlete, she will automatically tune in to sports-related ads. If a boy feels his identity is tied to a certain group (like being a Texan or a skater), ads and other messages that include or appeal to his groups will get noticed, especially if they utilize a kind of character (persona) or celebrity spokesperson that a member of the boy's identity group would relate to or admire (called an **ethos appeal**).[4]

See **Lesson 4C—Spokesperson**

THE TOOLS OF NUDGING

You might think that a seller attempting to influence so many potential customers into choosing his product might have to use massive and obvious tools, but in fact it is quite the opposite. We'll address noncommercial persuasive tools later,[5] but in general subtle nudging is more effective than an obvious shove, if only because we consumers aren't always aware of it and therefore put up no guard against it. When you also consider how we come to decision time often predisposed in one direction or with a set of values (with children instilled from parents), it doesn't take much to move us. Finally, it is the repetition within the **stalagmite effect** described above that is the key to persuasion as much as it is the force. Not to get too Zen, but a large wave may not be able to move a rock, but a hundred years of small, lapping ripples and that rock becomes sand.

See **Lesson 4D—How Many Reps Can You Do?**

The simplest nudge is by words. Take, for example, the power of "new and improved." If it's a product we already lean toward, then we'll certainly want it even more, even if we don't really know how it is better (or even why we need it to be better).[6]

See **Lesson 4E—Improve Improv**

THE VISION QUEST

What is the most dominant of our five human senses (leave it for the students to say "Spidey")? Many experts say the sense of smell is often the most linked with memory, but until smell-o-vision becomes a thing, it's not important for electronic advertising, and neither is taste or touch. That pretty much brings marketing down to sight and sound as the primary avenues for commercial persuasion, and of those two, by far, marketers try to earn dollars more through people's eyes than ears.

Vision is not only the main path of convincing someone; it is the overrider. No doubt we've all seen a movie where someone is forced to lie but tries to override their spoken words with visual cues (like saying "no" while vigorously nodding "yes" or saying they've "seen nothing" while using their eyes to direct a person to look somewhere in particular).

If visual nudging has always been important in advertising, it is more so today than it was one hundred years ago when magazine ads first flourished after the turn of the last century. With fewer avenues for information (and entertainment), ads back then were meant to be carefully read and considered after catching a person's eye. Today, with so many competitors vying for a person's attention—whether in print or online—an ad must have the visual appeal to catch someone in an instant and hold it long enough for a message to stick before they turn the page or click on the next link. Thus, the very composition of ads has changed to meet our shortness of attention and time.

See **Lesson 4F—A Family of One?**

See **Lesson 4G—Single-Frame Storytelling**

Specific visual cues, such as a spokesperson wearing a lab coat, tell us immediately they are an expert and therefore anything they say must be scientifically valid. Going more abstract, placing a product amid a pleasing visual can make the viewer look longer and feel more attuned to the ad. Even getting the customer into the brick-and-mortar store isn't always enough; customers may need that extra nudge to seal the deal and buy, so store and restaurant owners try to make their establishments visually appealing if not consumption-stimulating.

See **Lesson 4H — Buy Me, Buy It**

See **Lesson 4I — Eating Up the Decor**

Of course, the most central visual cue for a company is its **logo**, or symbol. The word "logo" is short for "logogram," meaning a sign in place of a word (like a peace sign). Companies like to use them because they are easier to see and recognize.

Think of traveling along the highway, looking for a place to eat. You could try to read the names of the restaurants to see if you should pull off, but a quick glance at the golden arches tells you what's there in an instant so you don't miss the exit, plus the visual hits you in your (hungry) gut. Companies spend lots of money on logos, and the ones that work best are the ones you can recognize even out of context. Of course, the logo is not effective unless it is placed where people look, but advertisers study that as well. They have an even better awareness of where the potential buyers are looking than the consumers themselves.[7]

See **Lesson 4J — LoGO!**

CHAPTER 4 ACCOMPANYING LESSONS

Lesson 4A — Is That Us?

Key Concepts
  Social forces nudging us
Special Materials/Media
  Computer to do research or magazines
Intro Questions/Thoughts for Students

- How can you know what life is like in another time or place? As a detective, what kinds of things might reflect how people lived or what they did?
- When archaeologists or historians talk about what the past was like, what do they look at?

Activity

Students pretend they are archaeologists who dig up our "lost civilization." They haven't yet translated our language, but they can look at the pictures and from that decide what life was like. You (the teacher) should have students look at magazines or online ads. From these, students assume that this is what life was like and present their findings to their fellow archaeologists.

The archaeologists should assume just about everyone did what the ads shows (why else would it be so popular?). For fun, they can also make "bad guesses" ("The people of the early 2000s had not yet invented individual bathtubs, but instead all bathed in big community bathtubs called swimming pools"). The teacher can also give one type of magazine (sports, entertainment, home decorating) to different groups to see how different the pictures of life are between them all.

Follow-up Questions/Discussions

- If you assume that whatever shown is what most people do, is it accurate? How many in your class actually do that or live that way? Do real archaeologists have the same problem?
- When you see a lot of ads that show you something you don't do or have, does that ever make you feel left out? Does it make you want to have or do whatever is shown? Is that the intent of the ad maker?
- When you see ads of what older kids do, does that make you want to do it? Do you remember ads or programs from when you were younger that showed you how life would be at your current age? Did it make you want to do it then?
- If ads are trying to get you to do or want something, what might they be leaving out, like the cost or maybe bad things that could happen?

Social Questions for Students

- If people tell you that "everyone" is doing something, or you are expected to want or to do something, is it OK to not want it? What can you do if you are not sure if something everyone says you should want or do is right for you?

Lesson 4B—Count on It

Key Concepts
   Media affecting point of view, ubiquity of media, brand impression
Special Materials/Media
   None
Intro Questions/Thoughts for Students

- What is an ad? What is a logo?
- How many ads do you think you see every day?
- How aware are you of when someone is trying to send you a message to influence your decisions? Do you think you catch more than 50 percent?

Activity

Have students choose a day to carry around a tally sheet. From the moment they wake up (writing down the time), have them record each logo or ad they see or hear as well as the time and manner (billboard, friend's shirt, etc.). How soon before they have seen or heard ten ads? Count seeing logos or hearing the brand name as an ad. Have students make a prediction beforehand as to the time it will take or how many brands they will encounter before noon. Twenty? Fifty? More in a whole day?

Students should include in their count and pay particularly close attention for when people mention a brand name, such as "I went to Starbucks this morning" or "Have you heard the new tune from . . . ," or are wearing a shirt or other clothing with a name or logo you can see. This is called **viral advertising** and in effect is getting the consumers to be advertisers for the product.

Follow-up Questions/Discussions

- Who had the most? Did anyone get ten before they left their bedroom? Did you take notice of any you weren't really aware of before?
- Do you think being exposed to that many ads has an effect even if we don't take notice of them?
- Some of the ads you encountered seemed accidental (such as driving by), but is it really an "accident" or was it placed there to wait for you and others to pass by and see it, like a highway road sign?
- How many of your tallies were from other people mentioning a brand or wearing it or referring you to an ad (viral advertising)? Do you think companies try to encourage this? How many brands do *you* advertise for? Some companies have actually paid kids to secretly promote their products by using/mentioning them to their friends. Would you be willing to secretly try to sell things to your friends (pretend you like something you don't) for money?
- Why do you think companies give away free stuff (with their name and logo on it)?
- How does all the advertising we see create a stalagmite effect? In what case would this "drip, drip" strategy work on people and when would it not? Could it influence you?

Social Questions for Students

- Can other invisible things all around us affect us, like moods, attitudes, or ways we treat each other? Can being positive or negative toward something (like school) or treating a person a particular way become "normalized" and thus expected of everyone? What if you heard all day that "John is a bad guy"? Might it eventually become your view of him? What can you do?

Lesson 4C — Spokesperson

Key Concepts
   Ethos in persuasion, endorsement as persuasion
Special Materials/Media
   Access to the Internet
Intro Questions/Thoughts for Students

- Have you ever seen a celebrity using or talking about a product or brand?
- If you see someone you admire doing something, does that make you want to do it? What if they are eating or drinking something? Does that make you want to eat or drink it?
- What kind of people influence your decisions? Do you listen more to athletes, scientists, or entertainers? How about wise elderly people? Why?

Activity

Find an ad where a famous person is shown using or endorsing (promoting) a product or service. For that ad, answer the following:

- Who is the spokesperson, and why are they famous?
- What is the product the person is endorsing?
- Is the product connected (such as sports equipment with an athlete) or unrelated (a soft drink with an athlete) to why the spokesperson is famous?
- Does the spokesperson make *you* more interested in the product? Why or why not?

Follow-up Questions/Discussions

- People say they are not influenced, but how many ads did you immediately think of with a famous spokesperson without even researching?
- Organize the spokespeople by categories, such as sportspeople, entertainers, politicians, or scientists. Are there any overwhelming categories? Why do you think there are more entertainers endorsing products than scientists? What kind of product could Einstein endorse?
- Are you more persuaded by a famous spokesperson endorsing a product or if the product is endorsed by someone like you (such as in an ad with a young person you don't know)? Does it depend on the kind of product?

Social Questions for Students

- Are there "trendsetters" in your school or group? Are there people whom others follow?
- What could you endorse that people might consider because you are recommending it? Have each person make an ad in which they are the spokesperson for their area of "expertise."

Lesson 4D—How Many Reps Can You Do?

Key Concepts
   Repetition as a sales technique
Special Materials/Media
   Access to ads
Intro Questions/Thoughts for Students

- Do your parents or teachers repeat things like instructions? Why do they do that? Do you think it helps?
- Do other people with messages, like advertisers, repeat themselves?

Activity

The teacher should choose a simple product that is well known, like a soft drink or fast-food chain. Students should then keep a tally sheet for one to three days and see how many times:

- they see an ad about the product;
- they hear about the product; and
- they see the product somewhere, like being held by another person or driving past a sign or store.

Follow-up Questions/Discussions

- If the products are already well known, why do they keep telling you about them?
- Advertising costs money, so why do they do it so much?
- Your tally sheet is how many times you were *aware* you saw/heard about the product. Do you think there were a lot more you didn't catch?
- Were you surprised at some of the times you saw/heard about the product?

Social Questions for Students

- How can we know what is the right number of times to repeat something so that we know we are heard but not so many times as to bother people?
- If you don't like people (like parents and teachers) repeating things to you, what can you do (maybe the first time it is said) to make it unlikely they have to repeat?

Lesson 4E — Improve Improv

Key Concepts
   Product improvement, **ergonomics** (designing products and systems to be most efficient for human use)
Special Materials/Media
   None
Intro Questions/Thoughts for Students

- What does it mean to "improve" a product?
- Is a product that is "more" or "new" always better? When you hear that a product that's been out for a while has been redone as "new," do you automatically assume it is improved or better?
- When a product is said to be "new" or "improved," does it always mean the product or can it mean the packaging?
- What is ergonomics?

Activity

The class is divided into groups. Taking turns, the teacher (or another group) calls out an everyday product (from pencils to cars). The team called upon then has two to five minutes to come up with a thirty-second ad they will act out that shows how the product has been redesigned or changed to be "new" or "improved." The teacher can decide if the improvement must be realistic or fantastical. The teacher can adjust the time allowed to suit the groups' time to prepare (longer time also affords a lesson in planning and cooperation).

Follow-up Questions/Discussions

- How many of the improvements would you consider to be an actual improvement, rather than a change just for change's sake?
- Can a company change a product too much? Might some people miss the old version? Are there any products (such as games) where you like an

older version better? Research the story of "New Coke" by the Coca-Cola company.
- Why do companies look to constantly upgrade and improve their product? If they have a winner, why change it?
- In the computer world, there always seem to be "upgrades." In computer games, there always seem to be add-ons one can buy. Why do you think companies do this, rather than sell all of it at once or wait until they can sell it all as a whole new product?

Social Questions for Students

- In what areas do you feel the need to always improve yourself? Why? Is it more for internal desire or because other people (such as parents) are telling you to improve? Is there a difference in motivation for you?

Lesson 4F—A Family of One?

Key Concepts
   Sample size, drawing a **hasty conclusion**, **stereotypes** and **sampling errors**
Special Materials/Media
   None
Intro Questions/Thoughts for Students

- Examples help us to understand something better, but how many samples are enough to get a good idea?
- What is the danger of not getting enough examples of something before drawing a conclusion?

Activity

The teacher can create an improper sample size in one of two ways:

- Case 1: The student must ask one family member what is there favorite thing to do or what would be a "perfect day."
- Case 2: The teacher calls out a time of day (8:30 am, 3:00 pm). Each student writes down what they were doing yesterday at that time.

The teacher collects the responses and tells the class:

- (for Case 1) that the school has hired an activities director and now every Wednesday the entire school will be doing this all day [read each], or

- (for Case 2) the school is hiring a new head of school who will be spending all day [read each] or that he will be your teacher next year and all you know about him is that he does this.

Kids discuss if each sounds good or bad.

Follow-up Questions/Discussions

- Some were funny, some were odd, some sounded bad. Did any of them sound good to do the whole time? Even if an activity sounded fun, what is the downside of doing it all day (such as not learning enough to get to the next grade)?
- What if we assumed that whatever the family member did, the student must like to do that as well? Would that be fair? Is one example of a family member enough to know what the student likes?
- For Case 2, can knowing what a person did one time tell you enough to know that person?

Social Questions for Students

- Have you ever had people judge you by one small incident? What can you do to correct what they think of you based on that?
- Maybe you have made a judgment about someone else based on too few examples. What does it mean to give someone "a second chance"? Think of someone you could give a second (or third or fourth) chance to and do so.

Lesson 4G—Single-Frame Storytelling

Key Concepts
  Visual ads as suggesting stories
Special Materials/Media
  Access to Internet
Intro Questions/Thoughts for Students

- Comic strips and comic books tell a story in several pictures, but can an entire story be told in a single picture? Often, ads drop you in the middle of a situation (such as a messy house but with a sparkling clean kitchen floor and a happy homeowner with a mop and Mr. Clean). You can figure out a lot of the background story (the kitchen was messy before, perhaps after making a big holiday meal, but was cleaned up easily) along with the ad's text (ad copy) that often adds to the narrative.

Activity

Provide students with an ad that seems to drop the viewer into a situation. Students should then write a paragraph that tells the story of the ad as a problem-and-solution format. Have them act it out as a skit.

Follow-up Questions/Discussion

- Did the class generally see the same ad as the same story? Are most of the stories built around a theme (such as problem-solution)? Who or what are the heroes of the ads?
- You can also look for two-picture ads that convey before/after or the perfect ideal and then the reality (usually wanting) and have students explain what happened between the two as a lesson in cause-effect and deductive reasoning.

Social Questions for Students

- How well can you estimate what another person is feeling just by looking at their expression? There are some online tests[8]; see if you can use them to correctly identify emotions by facial expressions.
- Great photography also drops you in the middle of a story. Look up the photos of Dorothea Lange, a famous photographer during the Great Depression. For one of her pictures (or someone else's), write a story about what happened to the people and what they are thinking. Being able to understand another's feelings, even by a picture, is called *empathy*.

Lesson 4H—Buy Me, Buy It

Key Concepts
    Product placement
Special Materials/Media
    Access to videos
Intro Questions/Thoughts for Students

- When watching a show, do you ever notice a product (such as a soft drink) sitting near the person or a logo? Perhaps you have a favorite YouTube celebrity and you notice what they are wearing or how their room is decorated. Do you think that is meant to influence you?

Activity

Students watch celebrities, either in interviews or when they have a nonfiction show (like on YouTube), and try to find products or logos in the picture. They may have to look around the room to see. They should also listen if a company or product (could be a new film, album, book, etc.) is mentioned. Finally, students should see if they can find an ad for that product that has that same celebrity in the ad.

Follow-up Questions/Discussions

- Was it hard to find products? Were some logos clear to see?
- Many TV shows black out logos or change product names (a famous TV show changed the Apple computer logo to a pear!), so why do you think some shows don't block out the logo or even mention it?

Social Questions for Students

- If someone is trying to get you to do something without directly telling you, is that OK? Is it better to just say, "I want you to do this"?
- Is it OK to want to do something or buy something or dress some way because someone you like does it?

Lesson 4I — Eating Up the Decor

Key Concepts
   Subconscious visual factors on consumerism, **ambience**
Special Materials/Media
   Visit to a restaurant; props in a classroom for a restaurant or access to Internet and printer
Intro Questions/Thoughts for Students

- What's your favorite restaurant? Why?
- We mostly choose restaurants by what we like to eat, which is of course based mostly on our senses of taste and smell, but do our other senses affect how "appetizing" the food is?
- A little-known fact is that restaurants like to keep their places cool because the cooler a body feels, the hungrier we will be (to generate heat calories). So can other senses, such as sight, also make us want to eat certain things?
- Have you ever been with someone who sees a restaurant and says, "That looks good!"?

Activity

Kids should try over a week to go to a restaurant at least once. While they are there, they should take notes on how what they see helps to sell food, including:

- pictures of food;
- decor that fits the kind of food (Italian, Thai, Mexican, etc.);
- placement of tables or sample foods;
- other nudges, such as sounds.

After their field work, kids should compare notes to look for:

- visual (and other) cues common to all kinds of restaurants and
- visual (and other) cues that are common to a particular kind of food.

As a follow-up fun activity, the teacher can call out a theme, either real (Greek) or fun (Martian), and the class must look on the Internet and print or make pictures to create a cafe that fits that theme. You can ask kids outside of the class to look at the different cafes (if you create multiple ones) and ask them to guess what is the theme and what kind of food they think is served there.

Follow-up Questions/Discussions

- Why do you think restaurants make sure their look matches the kind of food served?
- Restaurants can be expensive, so some people want not just food but an "experience." How does the decor help with this? Would you rather eat at a restaurant that has cheaper prices and no decorations? Did you notice a difference in decor between expensive restaurants and moderately priced ones? How so?

Social Questions for Students

- How much do we judge an event by the place where it happens rather than what goes on there? Is that fair?
- If someone who didn't know you walked into your room at home, what would they think about you? What impression would they get? What would appear to be your strengths, and what would appear to be things you needed to work on? Is it fair to judge you this way? Why or why not?

Lesson 4J — LoGO!

Key Concepts
   Power of logos

Special Materials/Media
   None (perhaps computer to find and create pictures [using a snipping tool])

Intro Questions/Thoughts for Students

- Why do companies use a logo, or symbol, rather than writing out their name?
- A logo often has a picture along with letters. Why do companies want to use a picture to represent them? Is the picture easier to remember or recognize? Does the picture imply something about the company?

Activity

Students are to create logos for themselves. The logo can be their name or initials or (and preferably) include a picture that they would want to represent them (soccer ball, a lion). The students should put their name on the back so that the teacher can display them all and have students see their own hall of logos (perhaps guessing which belongs to whom).

Follow-up Questions/Discussions

- Did the logos vary? Were some simple, others complex? Did it depend on whether the person was thinking about people recognizing the logo?
- Were any of the logos surprising, such as a student including a picture of something people didn't know about them?
- Logos for people is not new. In ancient Greece, soldiers from each city carried shields with similar designs so the other side could tell the soldiers were from Athens (owl on shield) or Sparta (Lambda letter). Later on, individual knights and families had logos, called coats of arms.

Social Questions for Students

- Can someone know all about you by just one thing (or picture) about you? Do you ever get tired of being known as "the soccer kid" or "the reader" even if it is something you are good at? Maybe redo the logo (or just write out) to show something you wish people knew about you but didn't.
- If we don't like being known for just one thing, maybe others don't either. In pairs or groups, interview other classmates and find out something you didn't know about them, such as a hobby or someplace they have been.

NOTES

1. Of course, some parents have to deal with the perceptive, vocal child who resists nudges and shoves back, seeing any choice as an invitation for a negotiated summit.

2. We will keep returning to the concept of aspirational buying throughout this book (see chapters 6 and 8). The concept is difficult for children to understand, however, as they have not yet experienced the reality (and conflict with their aspirations) of the older age. We do provide experiential lessons of the concept in the books for middle and high schoolers more, however, as they can look back and compare what they thought being older would be like (the media messages) with the reality.

3. "Under the radar" messaging is generally designed so as not to be noticed directly, or so the receiver isn't aware they are receiving messaging from professionals. For example, a marketing firm might hire kids to play with a toy (or give them out free) to "seed" interest by other children observing them.

4. It's interesting as well that, no matter how much a child (or even adult) fan acknowledges they root for the whole team, only one or two members of the team are recognizable or used as spokespeople in the community (or have their jerseys sold). See Lesson 9I regarding **logos** and **pathos appeals**, which, with **ethos appeal**, are the holy trinity of appeal techniques.

5. See chapter 9.

6. Teachers often learn to maintain silence as the hear about educational theory and approaches that are "reinvented" or "reimagined," even while they remember the exact same approach from a couple of years before.

7. There has been much speculation as to the custom of putting logos on the left side of a shirt, but generally the theories center on the left side being more visually demonstrative for the majority of people who are right-handed, either because the right side scrunches up when shaking hands while the left remains flat or because there is a broader display area on the button-less left side.

8. See, for example, https://socialintelligence.labinthewild.org/mite/, https://well.blogs.nytimes.com/2013/10/03/well-quiz-the-mind-behind-the-eyes/, or https://greatergood.berkeley.edu/quizzes/ei_quiz/take_quiz.

Chapter Five

Coolness

The Super Nudge

We don't want to speak on behalf of all those involved in economics, finance, and media literacy, but there is a certain irony in the profession: we are compelled to study "coolness" in all its forms more than perhaps any other academic discipline, yet we, as a group, were probably the folks least associated with coolness in our formative years! So far, we've looked at the standard tools (or tricks) for nudging consumers toward a particular choice in their seemingly "independent" decision making. The fact is, however, no other tool comes with more attachments, and no trick is more potent with younger consumers, than using the idea of something being "cool" to nudge people in its direction.

To understand coolness, let's go back to the late 1800s to a man with a cool name, Thorstein Veblen. Unfortunately for Veblen, he sacrificed any public perception of coolness by studying philosophy and then economics. At that time, economics would have stressed that a person purchases a product based purely on its utility,[1] or usefulness, and that such a person would consider the product's utility principally in light of price and quality in making his decision, a very rational process on all accounts.

Now, imagine Veblen, trained in this economic mindset, sitting in a park, watching people stroll by, when he sees and considers a well-dressed, able-bodied man strolling by with a well-appointed, highly polished walking stick. To Veblen's eye, the man is not in need of a walking stick, as he seems fit. So why then did this man of industry carry and, more to the point, purchase a cane? Without utility, the price and quality factors do not even matter. The man is apparently of a sound mind and seems successful in making financial decisions, as do many other wealthy men whom eagle-eyed Veblen has now noticed have also purchased walking sticks.

What, then, could be the reason for this? Undaunted by the confining walls of considering only sensible factors in decision making, our superhero economist Veblen the Vanquisher breaks through the boundaries of neoclassical economics to eventually come to the conclusion that the purchase was not done for a conscious, rational reason but for a conscious, *nonrational* one: to impress others. By utilizing a walking stick he does not need, our stroller sends the signal not only that his hands are free from labor to do as he pleases with them, but that he can afford to spend his money on unnecessary, ostentatious items.

Veblen coined a term for this kind of act, **conspicuous consumption**, in his seminal 1899 book *The Theory of the Leisure Class* and with this, in effect, launched the study of nonrational economic decision making (though to date the glory of being immortalized as an action figure still eludes him).

One could say that Veblen is the first to study the idea of doing things to be cool, but that motivation, even according to Veblen, has been around a lot longer. Going well back before Veblen, say about ten thousand years before him, to the dawn of civilization, let's consider two rival tribes called the *crunchies* and the *smoothies*. They both covet peanuts as a food source (the divide probably goes back that far), so the crunchies attack the smoothies to take their peanuts.

In the ensuing battle, one crunchy warrior, Jiffy, finds the king of the smoothies' ceremonial eating spoon, so he takes it. Being part of the captured goods, it is what people (notably pirates) called *booty*. The spoon has no practical use. It is too big and heavy, but Jiffy wants to keep it to show off what he captured so his fellow tribesmen will admire him. Veblen calls such an item **honorific booty**, or a thing acquired for the utility of admiration from others or feeling good about one's self for having it.

We can take this one step further, subdividing such goods into two kinds: **internal honorific booty**, or things that make us feel good for having them regardless of who knows (your *Lord of the Rings*–like "precious"), and **external honorific booty**, or the things that make us feel good because others see us with them and admire us for having them.

See **Lesson 5A—But What You Don't Know . . .**

See **Lesson 5B—But What I Need You to Know . . .**

Personal, long-term satisfaction may come more from internal honorific booty (especially when the things you possess are nontangibles like happiness, a sense of belonging, giving to others, or a sense of self), but it's external honorific booty that most often leads to what society deems "cool" (at least on the surface). In fact, an old synonym for cool (that actually predates it) is **panache**.

Panache means having a style or manner that stands out (for admiration), but it is its etymology (linguistic history) that is the giveaway. "Panache" comes from an old French word that meant a plume or ostrich feather that French military officers wore on their hats. Why did they wear such gaudy things? It was a privilege of rank, to stand out apart from one's own, non-officer troops (to say, "Respect me") and to stand out to the enemy aristocratic officers (perhaps to say, "Hey, don't hurt a fellow aristocrat; just take me prisoner and we'll talk"). That's what coolness got you back in the day!

Today, we don't wear plumes to stand out, but we wear many things to be cool, from certain labels to facial expressions and airs of attitude. We like to be seen in certain places, in certain ways, and with certain people. We know, rationally, that being near admired things doesn't make us better people, but who can resist that irrational pull to try to appropriate some admiration or have some coolness rub off?

Coolness would seem to be something the people decide, whether by collectively admiring and imitating someone with "it" (as was said of Clara Bow a century ago), attaching themselves to a consensus cool item (like Ray-Ban Wayfarers for sixty years), or joining in a movement or cultural vibe (the preppy look of the 1980s).

See **Lesson 5C—Work It**

Along with the people's choice, however, has come a host of marketers trying to "catch the wave" of emerging new trends (called **coolhunting**) to then try to influence, in turn, what is deemed cool by consumers. Along the way, marketers also discovered that one of the most powerful cool-nudgings is not just playing up the positiveness of being part of the cool but preying on the fear of isolation if one does not do so and is then left out.

See **Lesson 5D—Fad All Over**

One of the stranger aspects of cool is that cool kills itself. As soon as everyone is doing it, it no longer has that stand-out panache, and coolness has to move on to something else. Veblen referred to the process as **pecuniary emulation**, whereby the lower, less-monied classes imitate the wealthier ones' tastes and choices as best they can, which eventually drives the wealthy to find a new source of panache.

A wealthy person may have a limousine and driver, while below them a person might have a Bentley or other rare, high-end car but drive it themselves, below that a luxury car, then a mid-level car, economy car, down to economics teachers taking scooters to work! The *Freakonomics* folks similarly have a great study on how girls' names start off among the elite and then are adapted over the years by the lower socioeconomic classes until the upper classes move on. In any case, chasing cool is like chasing your shadow; it's short-lived and gone before you can catch it.

Children are also involved in an emulation process, but as discussed before, for them it is not just about emulating those with more money but those with more years on earth. Children will sing songs they hear even when they don't understand what they are singing about. How often does an elementary teacher hear a student sing a sad Taylor Swift (or other artist's) song about not having love and then shortly thereafter hears the same student exclaim "gross" because they came in physical contact with a child of another gender?

See **Lesson 5E—Lyrical Cool**

One particular aspect of cool that really stands out as a powerful nudger is being a rebel. It's a tough line to walk because coolness needs to be a natural, self-inherent trait one has regardless of one's environment, yet being a rebel requires being aware of and reactive to one's environment. And if you try too hard, even in rebellion, it isn't cool.

The high point of coolness, then, at least by pop-culture standards, is the person who goes their own way, but their way just happens to go against society's norms and can't be confined by them. It's the gal who just shrugs and says, "Sometimes you gotta break the rules," but is not in open defiance; it's just who she is. Then there's the "class clown," a rebel who hijacks a class, but are they truly "rebelling" or just acting out for their own needs, and is the class laughing *with him* (admiringly) or *at him*?[2]

See **Lesson 5F—Sometimes Ya Gotta Break the Rules . . .**

True cool rebels, then, don't shout at the system but walk their own path. They generally don't acquire external honorific booty (because that might show a concern for what others think of them), but they might acquire what could be called **negative honorific booty**, or things that society might not like but, because they are an independent trendsetter, the rebel does anyway and then garners admiration and personal pride (like Hippies sporting long hair), at least until they influence others and then move on.

Coolhunting, by either consumers or marketers, ends up being exhausting. For the price of quick and ephemeral popular approval, we have to spend lots of brainpower caring about not caring, watching what everyone else does to make sure we do something different to show we aren't affected by the majority. We can waste time, money, and resources, all in an ever-growing competition to outcool each other.

Perhaps the answer lies in an old Cold War term, MAD, which back then stood for *Mutual Assured Destruction*, and was the idea that either side could blow up the other, so let's just not and chill (and give that chilling the affectation *detente*). Today in the battle for coolness, perhaps we should adopt MAD, but this time, have it stand for *Mutual Assured Dweebness*: we're all awkward or uncool at times, so let's just chill; save the money, time, and effort; and maybe have an ice cream (no matter who makes it or where it's from).

See **Lesson 5G — Cool Starts Here**

See **Lesson 5H — Non-peer Pressure Is Really Cool; You Should Try It!**

See **Lesson 5I — You Knew the New You**

CHAPTER 5 ACCOMPANYING LESSONS

Lesson 5A — But What You Don't Know . . .

Key Concepts
  Internal honorific booty, **monetary value** versus **sentimental value**
Special Materials/Media
  None
Intro Questions/Thoughts for Students

- What does "having value" mean? What gives things "value"?
- What are the things that you value most, regardless of their monetary value? What is sentimental value?
- If you were going to help colonize Mars and could only take three things with you (NASA will provide all your necessities), what would they be? Why?

Activity

Students make a list of the three things that are most valuable to them (what would they take on a long mission to Mars) and why. They should then estimate the monetary value, such as if they were to sell it at a garage sale; how much do they think a stranger would pay for it? Make a list on a poster and compare total values. Students should also ask the same of their parents and bring in a list of their parents' most valuable possessions, like the Mars question above.

Follow-up Questions/Discussions

- Did the things on your list have more monetary or sentimental value?
- Were the items valued because they were associated with a person you know, associated with an event in your life, or somehow tied to you over a period of time (like a stuffed animal)?
- Were your parents' lists like yours? Were your parents guided by the same reasons as you were in keeping things?
- By looking at the entire class's lists of things and the reasons for valuing them, what are the most common reasons for people valuing things?

Social Questions for Students

- In the long run, what are the things that are important to you? How important is money in achieving them?

Lesson 5B — But What I Need You to Know . . .

Key Concepts
    External honorific booty, conspicuous consumption
Special Materials/Media
    Access to Internet
Intro Questions/Thoughts for Students

- What things or activities have value to you because people admire you for having or doing these things?
- How you can tell when someone is looked up to or admired?
- Do advertisers use the implied message "you will be admired" as a sales technique?

Activity

Students look for ads (or the teacher supplies them) that promote a product by implying that using the product will earn admiration or respect. It can be other people looking up at the user, or it might display the product-user standing out in a crowd or in a position of power with the product.

Follow-up Questions/Discussions

- Were there any particular kinds of products that used admiration in their ads?

- Were there any particular types of people in the ads being admired? Male or female? Younger or older? Any one kind of lifestyle (partier, businessperson, retired, etc.) that stood out?
- As a follow-up, pick ordinary objects in the room (like a stapler). Plan and then act out a thirty-second ad that shows a person being admired for having and using the ordinary object.

Social Questions for Students

- Do you admire some people for what they have rather than who they are? Is it admiration or jealousy?
- Is it OK to like someone because of something they own?
- Do you ever have something you want to show off? What about showing off skills as opposed to objects?

Lesson 5C — Work It

Key Concepts
    Coolness
Special Materials/Media
    Camera
Intro Questions/Thoughts for Students
    NOTE: As the students are the subjects here, it is best not to have introductory questions as that might influence the results.

Activity

The teacher has each student individually pose in the hallway for a photo (away from the other kids). The teacher should ask for a normal pic (maybe just stand or stand and smile) and then ask for a "cool pose."

Afterward, the teachers should put all the regular pics and cool pics up together and the class looks for similarities.[3]

Follow-up Questions/Discussions

- What general differences do you see between regular poses and cool poses?
- From the pics, can you come up with a general definition of a cool pose?
- How did you all learn what a cool pose is? From one TV show? From older brothers and sisters? From multiple places?
- If you have been taught that this kind of pose is cool, what else have you been taught is cool? Would you rather that you get to decide for yourself if something is cool?

Social Questions for Students

- Is it OK to think something is cool because everyone else thinks it's cool? Is it OK to *not* like it or to think something else is cooler?
- Imagine if people told you something was cool that you did not agree with (like not doing your homework). Act out ways you could say no to people trying to tell you it was cool to do.

Lesson 5D—Fad All Over

Key Concepts
　　Panache, conspicuous consumption, bandwagon effect, **fads**
Special Materials/Media
　　Internet, adults for interviewing
Intro Questions/Thoughts for Students

- Did you ever buy or own something in large part because "everyone else" had one or was doing it (like fidget spinners)? Did you ever want something before you even knew what it was because you didn't want to be left out? This is called the bandwagon effect and has been around a long time. Do you know of any historical fads (intense, temporary interest or popularity in a product or activity) that resulted from a bandwagon effect?

Activity

Students are to interview parents and grandparents and look online for fads that occurred in the past (from dance marathons of the 1930s, to hula hoops in the 1950s, to pet rocks of the 1970s, to the "preppy" look of the 1980s or "grunge" look in the 1990s). The class then constructs a giant wall-sized timeline of the fads complete with pictures. The class can vote which ones they think they would have tried back then or even try to recreate one (good luck finding a phone booth for phone booth stuffing).

Follow-up Questions/Discussions

- Does it seem like every generation (or decade) has a fad? Why is that?
- Do some fads of the past seem silly to you? Do you think people in the future will think yours are silly?
- Why do people spend money on a fad, especially one like pet rocks?
- How do you think marketers try to get their products to be part of a fad? How do they help spread the fad?
- Is helping a person to be accepted or liked an OK reason to buy something?

- Can you think of word or speaking fads? Research some (rhyming in the 1920s was the *bee's knees*; Hippie words in the 1960s were *groovy*; Valley girl speak in the 1980s was *totally tubular*!) and try them out now.

Social Questions for Students

- What are the current fads for your group? Are there fads that are particular to your school, area, or even state that is not so much a fad in the rest of the country? How did you learn of the fad?
- Does it make you especially proud if you are one of the first to be part of a fad? Why is that?
- Are there any fads that you would probably not do (wear, participate in) if it was not the "in thing to do"? You are probably not alone, so why do so many still do it?
- What might be the reason someone doesn't join a fad and does something different? What do you think when you see someone who doesn't go by what everyone else is doing?
- If there was a fad that you thought was bad or dangerous, what could you do? What if your friend wanted to try it?

Lesson 5E—Lyrical Cool

Key Concepts
Aspirational consumption (kids embracing things they do not understand)
Special Materials/Media
    Access to computer
Intro Questions/Thoughts for Students

- Is there anything you think is cool but that you don't quite understand yet, like a game or TV show?

Activity

This can be done in two parts (or you can just do one or the other).

- Part 1: Look for lyrics of popular old songs, such as "At the Hop" (1958), "I Am the Walrus" (1967), "Bohemian Rhapsody" (1975), "Sledgehammer" (1986), "Wannabe" (1996), and "Since U Been Gone" (2004). Play the songs and tell the kids these were cool in their day, and ask if the kids like them now. Print out or put up the lyrics and ask the kids what they think is the meaning of the lyrics ("At the Hop" is talking about being at a

dance, "Since U Been Gone" is talking about a woman feeling stronger on her own). Discuss if something has to be understood to be cool.
- Part 2: Look up popular songs today and ask kids if they know them. Again, ask if they understand the meaning of the song, such as breakups, or the slang.[4]

Follow-up Questions/Discussions

- Songs are generally written for older people (like in their twenties!). Can you understand the meaning of a song if you haven't been there yet?
- If you haven't had the same problem or experience a song talks about, can you still think it's cool?
- Are you deciding it's cool because other people say it's cool (it's popular) or because you think it's cool? Are both ways to decide something is cool OK?
- Lyrics also use slang or words and phrases popular at that time. What are some popular slang words from the past (gnarly, YOLO)? Would you use them today? What are slang phrases now?

Social Questions for Students

- Is there any danger in accepting something as cool because it is popular?
- Is it OK to say, "I don't get it," about something everyone else seems to understand? Do you think maybe others don't get it but are afraid to admit it? If you admit it, are you doing others a favor by speaking up?

Lesson 5F—Sometimes Ya Gotta Break the Rules . . .

Key Concepts
   Rebellion as coolness
Special Materials/Media
   Access to Internet
Intro Questions/Thoughts for Students

- What does it mean to be a "rebel"? It is usually defined as a person who goes against the rules, but what exactly does one have to rebel against to be one? Does it matter if the rebel is going against an unfairness (like people cheating) or something that is generally seen as OK (like obeying traffic lights)?

Activity

For as many movies or TV shows as students can think of, they should try to identify a character who is a rebel and fill in a chart like the one in table 5.1.

Follow-up Questions/Discussions

- Generally, do good guys rebel against bad rules and bad guys rebel against good rules?
- How many movies or shows can you find where the hero followed all the rules and won? If there are few, why is that so? What message is being sent?
- Can you admire a rule breaker who isn't trying to make things better for others but is just motivated because they don't want to obey the rule, like not go to school or be quiet during a performance?
- It almost always turns out OK in the end, but consider other possibilities when the rebel breaks a rule. What problems might have arisen? Why was the rule there in the first place? Did the rule breaker think about the people that might get hurt by his breaking the rule (such as driving crazy might lead to a crash)?

Social Questions for Students

- When is it OK to break rules in real life? Look up heroes such as Rosa Parks.
- Do you always know the consequences of what you do? For example, if you cut class, and the teacher sees you are missing, how many people will be called out to look for you? What if they had important things to do but then had to look for you?
- How many people do you rely on *not* to be rebels? What if the people at the power station or the food providers decided to be rebels and not work today?

Table 5.1.

Movie or TV show	Character	Rule they are rebelling against	How do they rebel?	How is the world better by their disobeying the rule?

Lesson 5G — Cool Starts Here

Key Concepts
Bandwagon effect, **peer pressure**, students following others
Special Materials/Media
None
Intro Questions/Thoughts for Students

- Have you ever done something because other kids do it? What about if people you admire do it?
- Have you ever started using words because you hear others use them, even if you are not sure what they mean?

Activity

The teacher makes up a word for something, such as *jiab* to mean *a surprise good thing* ("The teacher told us that, because we worked so hard in class, no homework for the weekend. That's so jiab!") or a nickname for a place ("Lunch is such a great time for me; I call the call the cafeteria my *loveland*!"). She can either start using the word or ask the class to, but then they should listen for if the word naturally spreads and is picked up by other students.[5]

Follow-up Questions/Discussions

- Did the word spread? Did people seem to naturally spread the word or start using it on purpose?
- Sometimes this experiment works (and the word catches on), and sometimes it does not. Either way, scientists learn from what happens. If the word did not catch on, what does that tell you about people adopting new words? What might be changed to make it more likely for the word to catch on?

Social Questions for Students

- When is it OK to use slang words and when is it not OK? Talking to friends? In a paragraph as homework?
- If you are talking with someone and they use a word you do not understand, how can you politely ask what it means? Act it out.
- If you use a word and a person seems to not understand it, how can you help them to understand without making them feel bad?

Lesson 5H—Non-peer Pressure Is Really Cool; You Should Try It!

Key Concepts
   Peer pressure and resistance to it
Special Materials/Media
   None
Intro Questions/Thoughts for Students

- What is peer pressure? How does it work?
- Would you ever do something you didn't enjoy just because everyone else was doing it?
- Would you do something you thought was bad if everyone else did it?

Activity

The teacher (or the class) makes up a new, silly fad (like wearing one shoe). The class has to make an ad that uses peer pressure ("Everyone is doing it!") to sell it. Then they should act out a skit where there are three groups:

- the ones who do the fad and want others to do it,
- those that don't want to do it (don't like it or think it's a bad idea), and
- those that could go either way.

The point of the skit is for those who don't want to do it to demonstrate ways to say no. Meanwhile, the third group should show how one can support others who don't want to do something even if they don't have an opinion (sometimes called being *an ally*).

Follow-up Questions/Discussions

- It's fun to be part of the in group doing something. Is it as much fun to say no?
- If you like a fad, how much should you try to get someone to do it before you should stop? Is there a certain number of times you should ask or tell them to do it? Can you say, "I like it, but it's OK if you don't"? Can you both like a fad and still be an ally for those who don't like it?
- How can a person be a good ally but still stay in the middle?

Social Questions for Students

- Have you ever been pressured to do something in real life? Does it help to have an ally?

Lesson 5I — You Knew the New You

Key Concepts
  Using "new and improved" to sell things
Special Materials/Media
  Poster board, markers
Intro Questions/Thoughts for Students

- What does it mean when an ad tells you something is "new and improved"?
- Why do we like it when things are "new and improved"?
- Are you in some ways a new and improved model over the "you" from a year ago (old model)?

Activity

Students are to make a poster or an ad that "sells" themselves as new and improved over the "old model" of a year ago. Why do they have more value? What new features do they have? What accessories do they come with? It might help for the teacher to show some "new and improved" ads, along with the excitement of the salesperson in saying it.

  Students then present their posters or act out their ads. Students can also do it for their parents.

Follow-up Questions/Discussions

- Was it hard to find ways you are new and improved? Why or why not? Would it help if others told you how they thought you were new and improved?
- Are there some things about you that aren't necessarily new and improved but you like them the way they are? What does the phrase "If it isn't broken, don't fix it" mean?
- Perhaps your class can, as a group, make a "new and improved" film to show the grade below you why your grade level will be great (new and improved) when they get there next year.

Social Questions for Students

- It's good to try to be better and better at something, but is it OK to remain "good enough" and enjoy where you are? Someone once said that, if you are always looking at the road up ahead, you can trip on the rock right at your feet. What do you think that means?

NOTES

1. See chapter 3 on utility.

2. And do these distinctions matter to the frazzled teacher who just needs to get through the lesson? One person once said that there is an important distinction between the "class clown" and the "class comedian." The former is the kid who stands up in class and makes noises with his hand in his armpit; the latter is the kid who whispered to the class clown that it would be really funny if he did that!

3. As always, when putting up pictures of the students, the teacher should caution the class that they should not make fun of any one student's pose or picture. They are social scientists there to look at the big picture of the data (and it's just rude!).

4. We highly recommend prescreening the songs, as lyrics can be, well, inappropriate for elementary kids.

5. If the teacher includes the class as observers/listeners, they need to use the word around school but in a natural way and not tell other kids about the experiment. They should report back to the teacher any time they hear someone outside of class use the word.

Chapter Six

Seeking Media Lit's Holy GRAIL

Consumer Demographics

Fun toy cars, a cool shade of eyeliner, and a great chair for an afternoon nap—all three are things that large groups of people would want and would pay money for (*consume*), but the members of those groups vary a great deal. Very few products are desired by everyone. Most sellers find they do better if they don't try to get everyone's money but instead target a particular group. This is well demonstrated by restaurants.

There are many kinds of food offered, from Italian, to Mexican, to steakhouses, to vegetarian cafes, but there are also differences in the atmosphere (family-friendly or trendy) and price (cheap or fine dining). No restaurant can do it all, and in fact we might actually be wary if we saw a restaurant advertise itself as the best Thai-Hamburger-Ethiopian-Vegan-Fine-Dining-Coffee-Waffle-House in the city!

Finding the right group of customers to sell to is called finding a **niche**. The term is taken from biology, where a niche is an environment or ecosystem where a species thrives, like seagulls on a coast or rattlesnakes in a desert. An economic niche is similar; it's that part of the general population of potential buyers (a *segment*) wherein a product will sell well and thus the consumers to whom a seller should pitch his or her goods. A seller who tries to sell comfortable lounge chairs to rambunctious six-year-olds will waste her money courting the wrong segment niche and probably be out of business in no time unless she switches and targets their tired parents. A seller, therefore, must have an understanding of population demographics.

See Lesson 6A — Scratch That Niche

In the end, a seller is on a quest, seeking the right segment of buyers who will raise their cups to receive the seller's offering. King Arthur and his knights were also on a quest, to find the Holy Grail, and while theirs was a nobler and less commercial pursuit, the parallel provides an easy way to remember five different ways sellers identify the right niche to target by finding their products' **GRAIL**:

G—gender
R—race or ethnicity
A—age or period in life (such as teens)
I—income level (economy, mid-level, or high-end)
L—lifestyle (sporty, trendy, living in a snowy place, etc.)

THE GRAIL AND ELEMENTARY EDUCATION

We take a lot of pride in developing the GRAIL system of segmentation analysis. Still, we recognize it is not developmentally or pedagogically appropriate for all students, especially at the elementary stage. By the time students are in high school, we have been able to just say, "What's the GRAIL sought here?" and students go to task. It requires, however, some awareness of social circumstances that elementary children may not be aware of nor that elementary teachers may be comfortable addressing in their particular classroom.

The disparity of social circumstances depending on one's race or ethnicity is a tough subject and may not even be welcomed in a classroom seeking to have students acculturated to not consider such factors for most topics.[1] Age is addressed more in the next chapter, but it is far easier for older students to look back and see the differences from where they were than asking elementary students to guess how they will be in the future. Income is difficult as well, as many elementary students have an undeveloped understanding of money, let alone class differences in living or ability to pay for things.

We therefore will touch on some of the segments here we think would be more acceptable and comprehensible to a majority of elementary students.[2]

Segments, Social Constructs, and Stereotypes

We adults know the real world is messy and often self-contradictory. To a child learning about it, that is confusing and perhaps scary (especially before the ability to consider things in the abstract). In teaching about the messy world of real life to elementary kids, one often finds two tendencies of children, either as a concrete way of thinking or as a data-management coping skill:

1. If a child hears a rule, it must be true and right.
2. Rules are rules, and exceptions should be absolutely avoided.

A child will tell you a red light means stop. Faced with a scenario in which someone is very ill—should a driver run a red light to get the sick person to the hospital?—the child can find themselves in the midst of a paralyzing moral conflict.

In the case of the GRAIL, we are presenting how marketers (who know what they are doing) often change their messaging based on what they consider "rules" of advertising ("girls like X; boys like Y") to appeal to the most members of the group they are speaking to. It is important here that we, and the teacher, emphasize that these rules are not "true and right" but are what marketers do.[3] People who don't conform to the marketer's GRAIL generalizations are neither bad nor wrong; perhaps it's the marketer's "rule" that should be evaluated!

Not all of these demographic segments are of concern to every product. Toothbrushes are fine for teeth belonging to a person of any race or gender, though some consider age when buying for children.

Even more, many of the perceived differences for segment targeting are more from social construct than from scientific evidence of who benefits. Yogurt is of the same nutritional value to men and women yet has been traditionally marketed (pitched) more to women. Many of these social constructs are changing, such as toys now being equally marketed to boys and girls. That may not stop some marketers from trying to convince consumers a product is specially made for them (and thus the consumer should pay more attention, if not dollars).

Another caution to remember is that segment niches categorize people in very general ways. Not all elderly people want to sit at home, nor do all teens want to party all night or follow the latest trend. We must remember that just because someone is part of a segment, they don't have to think like everyone in that segment. To assume everyone in a particular segment is the same is a marketing and, even more so, a social error called stereotyping.

See Lesson 6B—Brought to You in Stereotyping!

As consumers, we think of all this niche targeting (if we do at all) as producers passively watching people and collecting data, following some vague prime directive not to interfere with the indigenous population. It is important to remember, however, from a media lit standpoint—especially in regard to younger consumers—that the flow of information goes both ways.

If a little girl never sees another girl in an ad for toy cars, she may get the message that toy cars are not for her and that she should not want to play with them. Similarly, if a boy prefers arts to sports but only sees ads depicting boys playing sports, he might come to believe his preference for art is wrong, and he should play sports whether he likes it or not.

In the end, it is important that students both know how they are being categorized and then reflect on how much they wish to accept that categorization, so that the **feedback loop** stops or, rather, so that children can step off the merry-go-round of gender stereotyping if they wish. The more a consumer knows about him- or herself and accepts however they wish to self-categorize, the less they can be manipulated and compelled to consume products they really don't want or information that is false. The GRAIL challenges all consumers to see themselves from the outside in, asking, "What do marketers assume about me and how much of it is true?"

GENDER

Sociologists and psychologists still debate how much of gender differences (boys versus girls) are based on inherent biology or society, but we can all agree that much of the messaging communicates that some products and activities are particularly more suitable for one gender over the other. Messaging, as discussed previously, can be overt or, more likely, implied through things like the genders depicted in ads, the description of qualities of both the product and its consumer (tough or dainty), and even the colors (pink or blue) and music (thrashing guitar or light lilt) used in the ad.

The underlying questions such as "Where do our divisions in gender appeal come from?" or "How does/should the gender differentiation change?" are more suited to a psychology or sociology textbook than one on economics and media literacy, but no matter where one's opinion falls in whether gender preferences for certain goods is from biology or society, every individual should be able to choose whether to consume a good and should not be made to feel bad because he doesn't like what is traditionally favored by his gender or because she prefers a product or activity traditionally pitched to others.

See **Lesson 6C—Gender Sender**

See **Lesson 6D—Female and Male Persuasion**

RACE

In terms of race, America is in a transitional time. The United States historically has been majority white, and as such most media has been geared to white audiences, even if done by unintentionally using that perspective as the default mode for everyone. People of color were often cast, if they were represented at all, in supporting roles to a story about white people, even in ads.

Most products remain not targeted to a specific race or ethnicity. Still, marketers will highlight a particular race or ethnicity as a way of saying that their product is specially made with them in mind. It can be a general product, such as fast food, but with a special message to a group, or it can be a product made for the special needs of a member of a race or ethnicity (such as a hair-care product).[4]

See **Lesson 6E—Seeing Race**

AGE

Age is the most mutable, or changing, of the five aspects of the GRAIL. This can create a dilemma for marketers; once their brand is preferred by customers of a certain age group, say *tweens* (ten- to twelve-year-olds), is it better for the seller to "grow up" with their customers and then offer teen-oriented products or to stay in their niche and try to win over a new generation of customers? The marketer might think that they've already done the hard part of winning over a population, but then again, how much does that population still associate the brand with their younger, former selves at an age and time they would now prefer to leave behind to be more grown-up? On the other hand, a marketer can take the same product and give it a varied appeal simply by presenting the product with a pitch suitable for each age group targeted.

See **Lesson 6F—Jus4U**

One other special note about age is how often young people do not buy for the age group they are but for the age group they wish to be (aspirational buying). For marketers, this might lead them to not pitch to a child where they are in terms of emotional or psychological development but where the consumer wants to be.[5]

Can this be a problem? Some say it leads to **KGOY**, or **Kids Getting Older Younger**, wherein a younger consumer might rush to buy a product that they do not fully understand (such as a tween T-shirt that says, "Sexy!") or is even eventually led to or exposed to situations they are not ready to handle, be it watching something in media or partaking of it in real life. It also creates the possibility that young people will get a poor idea of future phases in life. As with fantasy, ads make for poor survey samplings of reality. Then again, even many adults are vulnerable to age-related fantasy messages, especially messages that say consumption of a product makes the adult young again!

INCOME

In the United States, people are taught that it is rude to inquire about or discuss income levels (one might note that in other countries, asking how much another person earns at their job is showing polite curiosity and interest). In fact, America prides itself on having a historically fluid class structure, creating the ideal of "rags to riches" opportunity.

As such, the norm is that differing income segments are often not overtly addressed but are appealed to by way of implicit language that then becomes understood by the audience (in politics, such indirect messaging has been labeled as *dog whistles*, implying that only certain segments can hear or be attuned to the call or real message). No one would ever say that their product is "for the rich," but they might say it is "high-end" or a "luxury" product (such as "gourmet" for food) and might be accompanied by visuals of affluent people using the product. At the other end of the economic scale, words like "budget" or "economy" might be used, again along with visuals to suit.

Of course, children often aren't faced with economic financial decision making. Combined with general American reluctance to talk about class diversity (and residential demographics where like-economic classes live together), children assume that their standard of living is usual, if not universal.[6]

See **Lesson 6G — Income in Code**

See **Lesson 6H — Price Is Right?**

LIFESTYLE

Lifestyle is the broadest of the categories, as it covers all the different ways we live our lives. It's the widest category and the one in which we get to have the most choice and power. A ten-year-old may be part of a single gender, race, age, and income segment, but she might be a part of one lifestyle on weekdays (student), another in the late afternoons (athlete), and a third on the weekends (a hobby such as surfing or collecting). It's not just what we do that determines lifestyle but also what communities we identify and associate with, based on categories such as religious beliefs or geography. In fact, there are so many facets to lifestyle, every person is probably a unique combination of all different lifestyles and accompanying degrees of participation and enjoyment of each.

Despite all the permutations and subcategories a single person's lifestyle provides, people often prefer simple labels, so we tend to put people in groups (even while we resist ourselves being put in a one-dimensional category). Perhaps it is acceptable to put people in general categories for certain activities (shopping for what they might like for a present), but we should never let such presumptions cloud us from seeing the total person.

See **Lesson 6I — Lifestyle Personal Shopper**

See **Lesson 6J — Circle Up**

CHAPTER 6 ACCOMPANYING LESSONS

Lesson 6A — Scratch That Niche

Key Concepts
   Concept of niche
Special Materials/Media
   Internet for research
Intro Questions/Thoughts for Students

- Why are there no polar bears on the warm coast? Why are there no mountain goats living in a city, or tropical fish in the snowy Himalaya mountains? Did the animals choose to live where they did? How do animals seem to end up in the "right place" for them to live?
- What kind of place or climate do you prefer? The mountains or the coast? Cold weather or warm?
- Look up what a niche is in biology, or the study of life.

Activity

The teacher should introduce the biological concept of niche to students, or generally the idea that an organism lives and survives where it does best. A polar bear thrives in the Arctic with its thick fur and protection against the cold but would not do well in the tropics.[7]

Once students understand the idea of niche, assign them in groups a certain niche (coast, mountains, tropics, etc.). You can also assign man-made niches like a big city or farm.

For each niche, students have to present two things:

1. an animal that thrives in that niche, explaining why that niche is good for the animal (or why the animal is equipped to do well in that niche), and
2. a product that they think sells well in that niche (snowshoes in the Arctic).

Follow-up Questions/Discussions

- How are the animal and your product related? Are both equipped to handle or deal with heat or rough terrain (ground)?
- Why do stores like Walmart, which are in many places, sell different things in different stores? Are they adapting to each store's niche?
- If you opened a store in your school, what products would fit in the niche that is your school? What would not sell well?

Social Questions for Students

- What is your niche in which you thrive? In the classroom? On the stage?
- What is a niche in which you don't do well? Is there anything you can do to better adapt to that niche?

Lesson 6B—Brought to You in Stereotyping!

Key Concepts
  Stereotyping, sampling error
Special Materials/Media
  Slips of paper
Intro Questions/Thoughts for Students

- Has anyone ever assumed you like or don't like something because other people similar to you like or don't like it?
- You are all about the same age, so is it fair to assume you are all the same in what you like or don't like?

Activity

The teacher has a list of questions:

1. What is your favorite food? What is your least favorite?
2. What is your favorite thing to do on the weekend?
3. What is a kind of music you like?
4. What is something you don't like to do?
5. What is your favorite sport or activity?

For each question, the teacher randomly calls on one student and writes that answer on the board. Then the teacher asks how many students agree and writes that down.

Follow-up Questions/Discussions

- What if someone assumed that each answer was true for everyone in the class, as they are all about the same age and are in the same class? Would that be true? Would that be fair?
- Assuming everyone is like one or two people with certain similar attributes is called stereotyping. What is the problem with doing it for the people who may not "fit" the stereotype?
- Why is stereotyping a problem for the person trying to learn, such as the person trying to get to know your class?
- Even if a majority (more than half) agree with the answer, why can stereotyping still be a problem, especially for those who don't agree?

Social Questions for Students

- How can we avoid stereotyping people by assuming they like/don't like something based on who they are or where they live?
- Is there something everyone around you likes or dislikes that you feel the opposite about? Maybe everyone should say some way they don't agree with the group, so that everyone can see even a group such as yours is made up of very different opinions and likes.

Lesson 6C—Gender Sender

Key Concepts
　Preconceptions based on gender
Special Materials/Media
　Picture of a horse or other animals
Intro Questions/Thoughts for Students

Picture of horse (ambiguous gender). *Joachim Marian Winkler, "Horse," Pixabay, https://pixabay.com/en/arabs-stallion-thoroughbred-arabian-1367173/.*

- When we look at something new, do we start with preconceived ideas? How much are we judging something based on things we have seen before or ideas we already have? Is that fair?

Activity

The teacher should show (or hand out) the picture of a horse to students and explain, "This is a picture of a male/female horse. Please look at it and tell me three adjectives you would use to describe it." Half of the students should be told it is a *male* horse and half should be told it's *female*, but everyone gets the *same* picture. If possible, the teacher should also note the gender of the student-respondent.

The class should then tabulate the results and assemble lists of the most common adjectives used to describe the perceived *male* horse and the perceived *female* horse. If possible, break down the responses also by the respondents' gender to see if there is a difference.

Follow-up Questions/Discussions

- Was there a significant difference in the adjectives used? If there were differences, did the different adjectives correspond to adjectives traditionally given to males (strong, bold) and females (graceful, beautiful)?
- Was there a difference between male and female respondents? Was one group more equal in their adjectives?
- Repeat the experiment with your parents and see if their results are similar (try not to give away what you are testing!).
- This is a modification of a 2002 experiment done with Spanish and German test subjects shown a picture of a bridge. (In Spanish, bridge, *el puente*, is male, and in German, *die brucke*, it is female.) The adjectives used by subjects to describe the bridge corresponded to traditional male/female adjectives, such as *beautiful, elegant, fragile,* and *pretty* for those who saw the bridge as female and *dangerous, strong, sturdy,* and *towering* for those who saw the bridge as male. We do not have male/female articles in English, but do we still think of some objects as male or female?

Social Questions for Students

- Do we pre-judge people to be a certain way by their gender or some other thing we know about them? Do we assume they are supposed to be one way or the other? When is that OK and when is it not?
- How do you feel when people assume you must be good or bad at something because of your gender (or another attribute)? Is there a difference if they assume something good or something bad about you?

Lesson 6D—Female and Male Persuasion

Key Concepts
 Gender roles and media
Special Materials/Media
 Videos or Internet
Intro Questions/Thoughts for Students

- Do you ever find yourself copying (imitating) what a favorite character in a story, movie, or TV show does?
- If you see a lot of small messages (nudges) to act a certain way, can all those messages add up, like drips of water make an ocean?
- Can you think of any rules that apply only to boys or girls? Why do we have those rules? Can you think of anything that "boys can get away with" or that "girls can get away with" that the other can't?

Activity

When it comes to a woman controlling her own destiny, we could put *Cinderella* at one end of a spectrum (passive heroine taken care of by her godmother until ultimately living happily ever after by being taken care of by a prince) and *Mulan* or *Wonder Woman* at the other (active heroine who defies tradition and society to save the country/world). Given this passive to active spectrum, where are other cartoon women that girls watch and see as role models? What about for boys?

Have students compile lists and re-watch children's shows to take note of the messages about boys and girls, what they should or should not do, and then create a "power line" or continuum and place characters along it after discussing where each should go.

- How many of the heroes and heroines are active versus passive changers of the world?
- How much does the male or female take the lead in a romance? Does the boy more often pursue the girl, the girl the boy, or is it about even?
- When one character falls in love (or even like) with another character, is it based on their object of desire's looks, talents (such as the sound of their voice), or personality (such as kindness)?
- How much does shopping/consumerism play a part in girls' vs. boys' lives in film?
- In the end ("happily ever after"), does the woman join the man's life (such as Ariel leaving her family and environment), the man join the woman's, or are they equal?

Follow-up Questions/Discussions

- What are the messages given to boys and girls about being a "new you"? Often in movies, the girl signifies her new self (new inside) by a new look outside (which is usually prettier or at least with more make-up, such as in *Grease*!). Is that true for boys?
- How do you think boys are affected by these messages to girls, or girls to the messages to boys?

Social Questions for Students

- Have heroes and heroines changed over time? How so? As a follow-up, interview a parent as to their impression of your favorite hero movie or show and its message.

Lesson 6E — Seeing Race

Key Concepts
    GRAIL, race in media
Special Materials/Media
    Access to photos
Intro Questions/Thoughts for Students

- Do we see things without even noticing we are seeing them?
- You sometimes hear people say, "I don't see race/color." What does that mean? Does it mean they don't see it or it doesn't matter to them?

Activity

The teacher should find a picture with lots of random objects in it plus people of different races (perhaps take a picture of a street scene). Students then have to try a "memory test" with the picture, looking at the picture for thirty seconds before being asked questions. Students should answer a list of five questions such as "What color was the wall?" but also include "How many people of color (non-white) were in the picture?" Tabulate results.

Follow-up Questions/Discussions

- How many of you noticed people of color in the picture?
- Did you get the question about the person's race right as often as the other questions?
- Do you think your parents would have similar results? Try it. If you do, why is it important not to give away beforehand that you are testing if they notice people of color?

Social Questions for Students

- How often do you "see" things about someone without being aware that you are seeing it?
- Is it rude to ask someone about their race or ethnicity out of curiosity? What is the best way to do so? Even if your question is politely phrased, might it annoy them (say, if it is the tenth time they are asked in a day)?

Lesson 6F — Jus4U

Key Concepts
    Segment niche, specialization of product regarding age
Special Materials/Media
    None (camera if you wish to have students film outside of class)

Intro Questions/Thoughts for Students

- What are products that people of different age groups all use? Are the ads used to sell it to each group the same?
- Are the reasons a kid buys something the same as the reasons why an older person would buy the same thing? Can you think of when the reasons might be different?

Activity

For a product or service, like shampoo or a restaurant, have groups design and act out TV ads (each thirty seconds to one minute) five ways:

- ad designed to sell to children
- ad designed to sell to middle-school kids
- ad designed to sell to teens
- ad designed to sell to parents (midthirties)
- ad designed to sell to senior citizens

This can be done in class with prep time or as an improv challenge (with three to four minutes between to change the ad).

In making the ads appeal to the different age groups, older elementary students can consider:

- *content* (the part of the experience emphasized) and
- *format* (pace, tone, language, camera angles, and action).

Follow-up Questions/Discussions

- How did the ads for the same product differ by age?
- How did you decide how to change the ad for that age group? Did students think about what that age group likes or does? Did you base it on someone you know that is that age?
- Would the way you did your ad appeal to everyone that age? Most people? Were you stereotyping?[8]
- There is an international award for best ads, the Clio (https://clios.com/). Take a look at the best ads of the past years. Why do you think they are considered the best? Do you agree?

Social Questions for Students

- Why do we like different things (or no longer like some things) as we get older?

- Do you like the same things you liked five years ago? Is it OK to still like some of those things (TV shows, fashion, toys)? What do you like now that you think you will not like in five years?
- Is it OK to change *whom* we like (or don't) in our circle of friends as we get older?
- Is it OK for a company (such as Starbucks) to say, "No kids allowed," in their stores?

Lesson 6G — Income in Code

Key Concepts
  Segment niche, specialization of product regarding income
Special Materials/Media
  Access to advertising
Intro Questions/Thoughts for Students

- In America, we consider it rude to openly talk about money, including how much some things cost or whether we have enough money to buy it. Instead, we use adjectives such as "luxury," "affordable," or "economy" to indicate how much something costs. Even when ads do say a price (such as automobile ads), such words are still used for reinforcement.
- What other words are used to imply how much something costs and who can afford it?

Activity

Have students watch (the teacher can find on YouTube) ads for products aimed at low- and high-income buyers, either by the product itself or the store. They should try to come up with a list of code words used to imply the economic level. Look also at the people, setting, music, and other common factors in making such ads.

Now, put into groups, they have been hired by a restaurant, *Chez Füd,* that sells many kinds of food (so the students can choose which to emphasize). They are to make two ads targeting each group without mentioning price but just using the cues like they saw from watching ads.

For their ads, they must fill out a plan sheet first that indicates:

  Word cues—
  Actor cues—
  Setting cues—

As the others in the class watch the ads, they must take note of how many of the planned cues they can see.

Follow-up Questions/Discussions

- Which of the two was easier to make? Which was harder? Why?
- Did you use any stereotypes about people of a certain income? Were they positive or negative? Were they fair? If someone of that economic group watched your ad, would they be persuaded or insulted?

Social Questions for Students

- It is socially unacceptable to make fun of someone because of their gender or race. Do you feel it is equally unacceptable to think less of someone or even make fun of them because of their family's income level? Why do kids who come from lower economic families sometimes feel embarrassed that they cannot afford some things (given they have as little control of their circumstances as someone born to an affluent family)?
- Have you ever been embarrassed to tell someone you can't afford to do something? What would you think if a friend told you they could not afford to do an activity you really wanted to do together?

Lesson 6H — Price Is Right?

Key Concepts
   Judging quality by price, rather than price by quality
Special Materials/Media
   Three kinds of cookies
Intro Questions/Thoughts for Students

- As buyers, we are supposed to decide if a product is worth the price, but do we sometimes let the price tell us what is good quality?
- If you go to the store and have to buy something you don't know anything about, would you buy the most expensive, least expensive, or middle-priced one? Why?

Activity

The class should set up a taste test for cookies (or the teacher can do it for the class). Explain to test subjects that they are needed to help decide which cookies the class will sell or have at a party. The three samples are labeled A, B, and C but should be introduced as "This is our basic," "This is our middle one," and "This is our ultra." Ask the people to rank the three. What the tasters do not know is that the cookies are from the same batch (or from comparable ones, like the same cookies but one is vanilla and one is chocolate).

Tabulate preference results.

Follow-up Questions/Discussions

- Did people prefer the high end more or all equally?
- What do you think would happen if you gave out actual expensive cookies as "low end" and cheaper ones as "high end"? Would people be able to tell?
- Instead of adjectives, what if you called the cookies by name brands known for low end, middle, and high end? Do you think that would affect people?

Social Questions for Students

- How often do we convince ourselves we like something or someone because we are "supposed" to like it/them more? Is that wrong? How can we better check ourselves to make sure we truly like something and not just because we are supposed to?
- Is there anything wrong with liking something because it costs more? What are the potential downsides of valuing things by how much they cost?
- Some people say they feel better about themselves when they "treat themselves" to expensive things. Is this OK? Do you feel better about yourself when you spend more money on yourself or someone spends a lot of money on a gift to you?
- How do you feel about people who try not to spend a lot? Do you think less about them?
- For all of the questions above, substitute "time" for the idea of "money"; are your answers the same?

Lesson 6I — Lifestyle Personal Shopper

Key Concepts
  Segment niche, specialization of product regarding lifestyle
Special Materials/Media
  Visit to a mall or online shopping
Intro Questions/Thoughts for Students

- While we tend to think of people in general groups (musicians, athletes, superheroes, friends) and thus similar to one another, there can be differences in personal tastes. How much do the tastes for a certain category of people overlap but still are different?

Activity

The class should think of a category of fictional characters (teens, wizards, superheroes, etc.). For that category, make a list of members, and then randomly assign pairs or groups of three students to be in charge of pretend shopping (but at real stores) for birthday gifts for that fictional character. They must find:

- one gift related to the character being a member of that category and
- one gift that is uniquely personal to that character's way of life.

You have a *total* budget of $100.
 Each group must make a presentation of what they would have bought and why.

Follow-up Questions/Discussions

- Was it harder to buy the category gift or the personal gift?
- Between the groups, was there more similarity between the category gifts or the personal gifts?
- How do the gifts show the characters are similar and different?
- Did you find things at one particular store, with one brand, or in many places? Which real-life store would be your character's favorite?
- If you were doing this for nonfictional characters (such as your teachers), do different stores/brands cater to their different lifestyles?

Social Questions for Students

- Are there assumptions you make about a person because they wear or use a certain brand?
- Do you feel better about yourself or your "look" when you wear a particular brand? Why?
- Do you feel better more often when you wear what most of your friends are wearing or when you have on something very different that makes you stand out?
- To be part of a group, how much should a person be willing to change themselves?

Lesson 6J—Circle Up

Key Concepts
 Lifestyle niche, figuring out one's own lifestyle niche
Special Materials/Media

Copies of Venn diagram below
Intro Questions/Thoughts for Students

- How do you fill in the blank, "I'm a _____ person"?
- How do you think your family would answer that question for you?
- How do you think a teacher on the first day of class might answer that for you, based on her first impression of you?

Activity

1. Each person should fill out the Venn diagram below as to what describes them.
2. Afterward, students should turn them in with their names on the back. The teacher can then post them and have students guess which diagram belongs to which student.
3. Alternatively, students can exchange papers and interview each other as to why they put what they did.
4. Afterward, students should get feedback, such as a list of "I didn't know you _____" related to what they put.

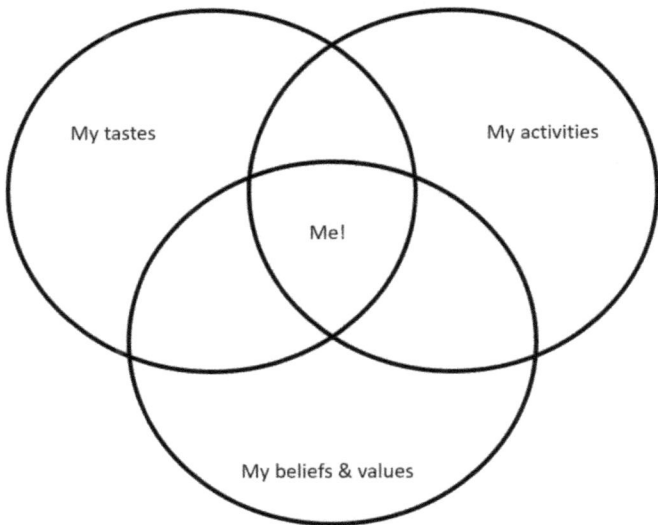

Follow-up Questions/Discussions

- Did people know which was yours right away, or were they not sure? Which way do you like it better, being an "open book" or a person of mystery?

- Which of your three choices were well-known by others? Which ones surprised people?
- Students should look back at their original "I'm a _____ person" and decide if they want to keep it as is or revise it. Either way, each student might then get two minutes to stand up and "introduce himself or herself" to the class by their lifestyle.

Social Questions for Students

- Some people don't like to share a lot of things about themselves. How can we respect the privacy of others but still get to know them?
- Were you surprised to find you had something in common with a particular person, maybe someone you don't normally hang around with?

NOTES

1. We certainly believe such disparities exist and need to be examined and discussed by students; we are just saying here that we leave it to elementary teachers if their students are ready for the topic.

2. For a more in-depth examination and lessons regarding the GRAIL segments, please see *Middle Schoolers, Meet Media Literacy* or even *High Schoolers, Meet Media Literacy* for advanced lessons on these segments.

3. The greater question—how much of these generalizations by marketers are a mere reflection of what society is and how much do what marketers say help create or perpetuate these distinctions—is addressed later in the book as the topic of a feedback loop.

4. And we will leave it here with having elementary students merely take note of race in messaging. As for the next step of drawing conclusions from the observations, we leave it to the teacher or, again, refer you to the middle- and high-school editions of this book series.

5. See also chapter 7.

6. See note 4, as we will leave conclusions about income disparity to the more advanced books in the series. Generally, however, we have found that it's the children of lower economically situated families that are more aware of socioeconomic differences.

7. Of course, this includes the process of adaptation to an environment through natural selection, but we are keeping this simple as it is an analogy.

8. See Lesson 6B.

Chapter Seven

An Age-Old Question

Age and Consumerism

If you have any recollection of your elementary school days, or have ever taught math, then chances are you know that six is afraid of seven . . . because seven *ate* nine! If this is new to you, we can pause while you consider the philosophical and social implications of cannibal numbers, but for the rest, why is that joke no longer funny? Most will tell you that the joke got old, but like a man in an Einstein problem watching a clock on a train moving at the speed of light, it's relative; it's less that the joke got old than *we* got old!

As we explored last chapter, we consumers can be segmented in five ways, collectively called the GRAIL. Each has their own special issues, but the age category is special because it's the one guaranteed to change. Biologists may roll their eyes at the idea that our cells regenerate every seven years, and thus we are "new people," but the fact is that biological maturation and change, combined with life experiences over time, create a new "you," at least in world perspective. The ancient Greek philosopher Heraclitus stated that one can never step in the same river twice because the river constantly changes, but it's also in many ways a new you doing the stepping.

We'll leave further philosophy to our toga-clad colleagues, but for our purposes, the concept of perpetual change deserves special attention because how the world's messages to people, and how people in turn process those messages, change with age. Whether it's a product (a "good" car) or a message ("good" people), we process it differently at six than at sixteen, twenty-six, or eighty-six.

THE CENTRICS

A popular ad once asked, "What would you do for a Klondike bar?" Before that, a spokesperson could be heard saying he'd "walk a mile for a Camel [cigarette]." What these two ads and many others touch upon is that we all have weaknesses; there are just some things folks have to have and would do just about anything to get.

While such ads acknowledge our physical cravings for things like sweets and nicotine, what they insidiously don't mention is that they are simultaneously playing on consumers' invisible, yet just as strong, emotional needs. Abraham Maslow famously published what he perceived as the *hierarchy of people's needs* in his 1943 paper "A Theory of Human Motivation." It would take a whole separate book to explain Maslow's hierarchy in detail, but his theory in a pyramid-shaped nutshell is that all human beings have similar needs (figure 7.1).

As Maslow describes it, the higher, more cognitive and emotional needs rest on a base of physiological and practical needs being first met. In general, we can say that the lower, base needs make living achievable, while the higher needs make life worthwhile. The media persuaders, whether in ads for cars or in campaign speeches, often format their appeals to say that our needs will be met by consumption of their product or agreement with their ideas.[1]

Each of us is a unique combination of GRAIL categories, yet we all need a "sense of belonging," even if that sense varies from person to person. One person's idea of "belonging" may be thinking of cuddling with a life partner,

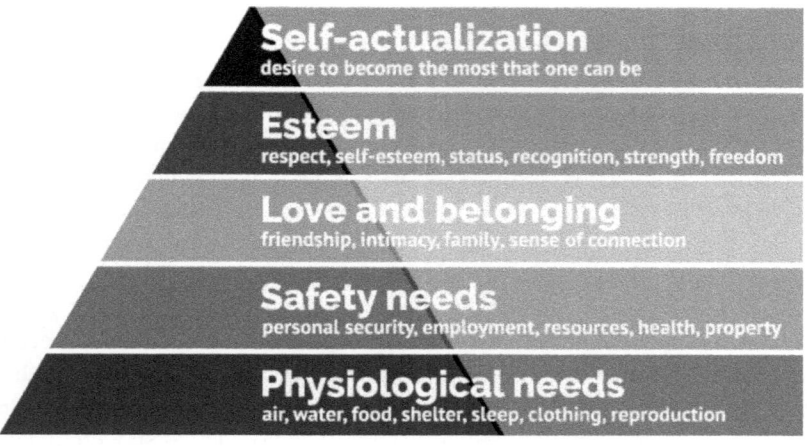

Figure 7.1. Maslow's Hierarchy of Needs pyramid. *Saul McLeod, "Maslow's Hierarchy of Needs," Simply Psychology, https://www.simplypsychology.org/maslow.html.*

while another may think of hanging out with a peer group, while still another may think of a team project achieving some never-before-realized breakthrough (such as a device that keeps a cat from waking up people at 4:00 am because it's hungry or lonely or just because it's a cat).

Still, research has found that there are some commonalities and that these commonalities can generally be leveled by age group. These common needs by age have been variously named, but here we shall call them **centrics**,[2] or the emotional and psychological needs of a particular age group. They are the sunshine that the plant grows toward, even if the direction from which the sunlight comes changes over the seasons. A tween's incontrovertibly cool T-shirt is yesterday's embarrassment once she is a teen, and perhaps a nostalgic remembrance once she is an adult.

Much of the work in identifying youth centrics was done and continues to be done by child, developmental, and adolescent psychologists. It is noteworthy, however, that leaning over the shoulders of these researchers (who do it to help children) are marketers and purveyors of information, looking for the perfect appeal to a centric that will make their message be gladly ingested. This is why teachers need to help students realize what those centrics are at a given stage, not so that students will refuse to satisfy that craving, but to be in better touch with it so as to make a healthier choice in satisfying it. We all crave sweets, but good nutrition information might make us reach for sweet fruit rather than candy to satisfy the craving, and we'll all live better for it.

CHILDREN'S CENTRICS

Regarding the centrics, or points of appeal, American children can be said to have three. First, they want the love and approval of their parents, teachers, and friends. To obtain this validation, children often imitate and adopt the identity, views, and behaviors of their immediate group as their own, so that they can feel a member of a protected tribe, as it were. They also may do so because there is simply no other example for them to see, such that theirs is not so much a choice to follow the dominant norm but an acceptance of what they perceive as the sole existent way to act and think. From a marketing and messaging point of view, a child can be encouraged to want a certain product, do a certain activity, or espouse a certain view by sending the child the message that doing so will give them that sense of *belonging*.

See **Lesson 7A — Fun Me Downs**

See **Lesson 7B — Love to Be Loved by You**

A second centric for kids is fun—plain and simple *fun*. Whether learning or relaxing, kids respond better to information pitched to them if it is presented in an engaging and entertaining way. Even if the thing itself (such as brushing teeth) is not inherently a joy of life, turning it into a game or wrapping the event in colors and music (such as musical toothbrushes) will draw kids into whatever message is being promoted. In 2002, a convention centered on Advertising and Promoting to Kids (APK) in New York even featured a session titled *Owning Fun! Reaching Kids through Product Innovation, Package Design and Brand Graphics*; and you thought fun was for everyone to own and share![3]

See **Lesson 7C — Boring into Fun**

The third centric available for utilization as a delivery tool for messaging to children is their desire to be grown up. We keep circling back to this, as it is a very strong motivator for children, but from an early age, kids want to dress up, be big, and enjoy all the perks of adulthood (until they hear about taxes, mortgages, and how the plumbing always breaks when you're away from the house). So much do kids want to hang with the big boys that they will consume, even gulp down, anything that older, more respected people (often siblings) consume, even if they don't understand it themselves.

This phenomenon is called aspirational buying[4] and can be easily exploited to get kids to advocate things they don't yet comprehend (such as T-shirts with messages with sweeping [and usually negative] generalizations about gender or homework or needing spa and shopping days) or do not realize the implications of (such as saying, "All _____ people are bad"). At the same APK convention mentioned above, the keynote address was titled *Emotional Branding for Kids: Creating Lifelong Consumers*. One expects parents would take umbrage at strangers devising how to brand their children.

With all three centrics, it's preferable to say that messages *convey* them rather than *depict* them. *Depict* really just means the author or artist is showing what they are thinking, regardless of whether the viewer or reader gets the message. *Convey*, on the other hand, is to carry something from one point to another, or share one person's idea with another. If the viewer or reader does not get the message of belonging, fun, or aspiration, then the idea was not conveyed and the message was a failure, like passing a basketball that goes out of bounds. In the end, it's not the messages depicted that have an impact; it's the ones that are conveyed.

See **Lesson 7D — Schooling You in Ads**

CHAPTER 7 ACCOMPANYING LESSONS

Lesson 7A — Fun Me Downs

Key Concepts
  Children's Centric of belonging, indirect messaging from parents, cultural (tacit) pressure
Special Materials/Media
  Access to Internet for research
Intro Questions/Thoughts for Students

- Were you given any toys or games, or introduced to them, by parents or older siblings who said, "I loved this as a kid!"?
- Did you ever feel pressure, even if it was not stated, to try or do something because it had been enjoyed by others before? Did you enjoy it?

Activity

Students think of toys or games that they had that have been around for a long time (if they cannot think of one, use Barbie dolls or construction sets). For whatever they pick, they should research the history of that toy: when it was invented, popularity, and how it looked and changed over the years. If it has been changed since they played with it, what are those changes? Students can then make a timeline of that toy, including placing their time playing with the toy on it. If their parents played with the toy or engaged in the activity, the student should place their parents in the timeline.

As a further challenge, students should imagine and design the "next generation" of that toy. What will it look like (or what extra features do they imagine it will have) in twenty years?

Follow-up Questions/Discussions

- If you enjoy that toy or activity, was part of the enjoyment knowing that you were doing something your parents (or older siblings) did?
- Were there any toys or activities handed down to you that you did not like? What happened? Did the older person try to talk you into liking it or "giving it another try"?
- Were you surprised by any of the changes of your toy over the years?
- As a follow-up activity, imagine five thousand years from now, archaeologists dig up the toys you have in your room. They don't know you, but what might they conclude about you, both rightly (from the game of

Trouble, this kid liked to compete for fun) or wrongly (from Mouse Trap, this kid had a mouse problem in his bedroom or was training to be a professional mouse catcher)?

Social Questions for Students

- Tacit pressure is when you are not directly told to do something, but the circumstances try to nudge you to do it. If you walk into a library talking, but then seeing people staring at you, you stop; this is tacit pressure, as no one directly told you to stop, but you got the message. Have you ever experienced tacit pressure to do or not do something?

Lesson 7B—Love to Be Loved by You

Key Concepts
   Children's centric of belonging
Special Materials/Media
   Access to ads, TV shows, or other media
Intro Questions/Thoughts for Students

- How do your parents and teachers show they approve or like what you are doing or like a decision you have made?
- How do your parents or teachers communicate to you what they would like you to do next?
- When your parents or teachers say they like what you are doing, does that make you want to do it more?

Activity

After generating the list as a class of ways adults show approval for what a child does (such as compliments, giving rewards, or hugging and other signs of affection), the students should look for TV shows or ads where they see parents or teachers doing this. Each student should try to find three examples (table 7.1).

Table 7.1.

Where did you see this? Ad? TV show?	What did the child do?	How did parents or teachers show approval?

Follow-up Questions/Discussions

- Do your parents and teachers show approval the way it is shown in the ads or on TV? How is it similar, and how is it different?
- Some ads show parents or teachers approving of a child who is using their product (such as everyone playing the game together). Why do you think the ad shows this? Does it make you want to try the product?

Social Questions for Students

- Is it OK to do something you don't like to do in order to get other kids to like you? What if you think what you need to do is wrong?
- If someone says, "I'll be your friend if you do this for me," what can you say in response?

Lesson 7C—Boring into Fun

Key Concepts
   Children's centric of fun
Special Materials/Media
   None
Intro Questions/Thoughts for Students

- What are things you have to do but that you think are boring?
- Do you have any strategies for turning boring activities or times into fun ones?

Activity

The class should generate a list of boring activities or circumstances. In groups the children are tasked with making a thirty-second ad/skit that makes the activity fun and "sells" the activity or circumstance. It has to be realistic (you can imagine there are Martians while waiting in the doctor's office, but there can't actually *be* Martians).

Follow-up Questions/Discussions

- What were the common ways people made something fun? Having a group say it was fun? Doing it together? Turning it into a competition?
- Do you think your skits might get someone who never was in that boring situation or activity to want to try it?

- Do advertisers do the same thing? Have you ever bought a toy or gone to a place because it was "sold" to you as being fun, but it turned out not to be so?

Social Questions for Students

- Some say that if everything or every place is boring or not fun, it's not the places; it's the person! How can we make sure we get the most enjoyment, if not fun, out of everything, including the things we have to do, like chores, waiting, or homework?

Lesson 7D—Schooling You in Ads

Key Concepts
 Advertising to children, establishing a brand as the **norm**
Special Materials/Media
 None (except a walk around the school)
Intro Questions/Thoughts for Students

- How often do you see ads for things? Are there ads you see so often you don't even really see them anymore?

Activity

Students should walk around their school with a tally sheet (table 7.2):
 As they walk around, each student should try to take note of all brands and logos that they see. The students should look for three types:

- brands and logos displayed by other children (such as on clothing or on their lunchbox);
- brands and logos displayed directly by the company (billboard); and
- brands and logos that are displayed through the school (signs, scoreboards, lunchroom food, vending machines, lesson plans, busses, etc.).

Table 7.2.

What is it an ad for?	Displayed by another student	Displayed by school	Displayed by product maker

Follow-up Questions/Discussions

- What was the most common source for the ads: the companies, other kids, or the school?
- If children don't have a lot of money, why is it worth it for companies to advertise to them?

Social Questions for Students

- Some of the ads have been there for a while, but maybe you just now noticed them because you were asked to. This is called using "fresh eyes." What other things may you be missing because you see them (but don't really look at them) every day?
- Are there some people that you should look at with "fresh eyes" to maybe reappreciate them?

NOTES

1. One also sees this in political messaging through fearmongering, or the assertion that support, let alone a victory, of the messenger's opponent will threaten the people's base needs, such as safety and security. This is really just an adult version of the "or else!" threat to children.

2. The first people to have coined the term "centrics" in terms of marketing motivators may have been David Siegel, Timothy Coffey, and Gregory Livingston in their book *The Great Tween Buying Machine: Marketing to Today's Tweens* (Ithaca, NY: Paramount Market Publishing, 2001). They defined centrics, at least regarding tweens, as the "core drivers that motivate . . . behavior" (50). We use it here similarly, except with more focus on such "drivers" that then become vulnerabilities by which media and messaging might resonate, persuade, and perhaps even manipulate us, for good or for bad.

3. An interesting contrast is that, whereas older children (tweens, teens) respond to coolness pitches because they want to be part of this amorphous thing called "coolness" (whether or not they personally like it), children want to be cool only if it is fun to be so, which in essence means children are savvier consumers than the older ones, as they are looking at coolness for its personal utility rather than its panache. See chapter 5 on coolness and panache.

4. See chapter 6 on related topics.

Chapter Eight

Child's Play or Child's Pay?

Children, Consumerism, and Media

The authors of this book are Texans. That might not seem important to you, but it is in this context.[1] An important rule for Texans is to never cut to the chase when a story can first be told (that we tell stories mainly about dead people is what qualified us to be classified as history teachers).

So, way back at the turn of the millennium, one of us was watching a certain kid's cable channel (we won't mouse around and tell you which one, even if you are all ears) with his six-year-old son (whom we will call "Ben" to avoid family embarrassment). Ben loved this channel, including a show called *Movie Surfers*, in which kids seemingly reviewed movies that were almost always made by the movie production arm (or other ear) of this corporate conglomerate.

On this particular episode, the kid-reviewers were discussing a movie just released that, frankly, had horrible reviews from independent sources, with one saying they wanted to know from whom to demand the ninety minutes of his life back. Nevertheless, the kids on the show *loved* the movie and raved about it excitedly. Ben, not wanting to miss out on this childhood phantasm of fun, turned and said, "Dad, we've *got* to go see it!"

Dad, being the wise economics teacher who wanted his child to understand that these supposedly earnest children were shills for a corporation bent on taking his future college funds, asked, "Ben, why do you think these kids are telling the truth?" Ben thought for a moment—and then teared up in world-crashing panic as he said, "But why would other kids not tell the truth? Are they *lying* to me?"

An important lesson was learned that day . . . by the dad: never introduce thoughtful but undermining questions about a child's favorite show, or at least do not pull back the curtain revealing the man behind it too soon (and further to immediately minimize family angst by taking Ben to see said movie, for which he gave it a grade of thoroughly "meh"). On the other hand, the story also illustrates that children should not be thought of as just future players in a marketers versus media lit game; they are playing the game *now*, and they are playing against professionals without even knowing it.

THE GODFATHER OF CHILDREN'S MARKETING

Meanwhile, back in Texas, we are aware that some think of our education system as something we do to kill time between weekend football, but many breakthroughs have come out of our universities. One professor from Texas A&M, however, remains very controversial in his twenty-seven-year-old insights regarding children and media lit.

In 1992, James McNeal, a marketing professor at Texas A&M, published a seminal book, *Kids as Customers*,[2] which laid out how marketing and messaging can be effectively used in regard to the under-ten set. Many marketers grabbed up a copy and still see it as a how-to guide to persuade children. Media lit people, on the other hand, see it as an insight into the other team's playbook, and herein it will be used to devise a prevent defense (see, as Texans, we couldn't stay away from football that long!).

McNeal considered children to be part of three markets: current customers, influencers on their parents' decisions (sometimes called "the nag factor"), and future consumers who will hopefully have a lot more buying power once they are adults with tastes influenced from childhood. Thus, according to McNeal, winning the child market can yield up to three returns on an investment.

See **Lesson 8A—3N1**

See **Lesson 8B—It's a Family Affair**

Savvy adult advertisers and other messengers preying on kids in any of the three ways described above is an unfair fight, but perhaps the most insidious of the three is the "nag factor," as it not only insinuates advertisers into the parent-child relationship (and makes it a child/advertiser vs. parent two-on-one), but often does so by undermining the child's trust in parents' wisdom and guidance, even as to things like nutrition or whether a purchase is economically a good deal.[3]

See **Lesson 8C—Playing Dumb**

Beyond pure marketing of products, McNeal's observations lead to two further insights in the field of media lit. First, whatever McNeal said about kids as consumers of tangible goods, including the three-markets-in-one, also applies to children as receivers of ideas and value messages. This is even truer today than in McNeal's time, with so much media saturation and so many avenues for messaging to be delivered to children.

See **Lesson 8D—About Face**

See **Lesson 8E—Political Stick Figures**

Second, as children are already desired and sought after by marketers, it is necessary they be educated as early as possible so as to be discriminating consumers of products and information (never forgetting that parents remain the gatekeepers as much as possible).

Sellers will call it **market penetration**, or merely informing potential consumers of choices, but when looked at from a media lit point of view, it could also be called colonizing our children and our future. Or, if you want it straight from the marketers' mouths, consider the following quotes as reported by Gary Ruskin in his 2003 article, "Why They Whine: How Corporations Prey on Our Children"[4]:

- *Children should be viewed as economic resources to be mined.*
- *Children are the brightest star in the consumer constellation.*
- *If you own this child at an early age, you can own this child for years to come.*
- *If you tell [children] to buy something, they are resistant. But if you tell them that they'll be a dork if they don't, you've got their attention. You open up emotional vulnerabilities, and it's very easy to do with kids because they're the most emotionally vulnerable.*

See **Lesson 8F—Drawing a Conclusion**

See **Lesson 8G—Little Big Things**

See **Lesson 8H—Breaking Good**

FINANCIAL LITERACY

We discussed in an earlier chapter the idea of nudging and how children are specifically susceptible to being nudged, either in a bad direction or a good one. Building on McNeal, good habits instilled in children can lead to life-long and exponential benefits throughout the students' lives. Speaking of nudging people in their decision making, there is a growing interest in making sure that our children come into adulthood not only media literate but financially literate. Though they are well-educated and well-paid, "Millennials" lament that, as they enter adulthood on their own, they somehow were never prepared for how to handle the money they earn or how to hold onto it.

They also are emerging with more debt than other generations previously, owing to everything from college loans to having been made available to general marketing, credit cards, and other buy-now-pay-later offers (with compounded interest) by predatory companies who preyed upon their naiveté when they were young.[5]

The path to financial success may be wider for today's youth, but there are also more potholes that can upend a financial plan. Even while many start with greater debt to pay off (in effect earning their first few years' paychecks for their college/loan institution rather than for themselves), the collective ethos is no longer to work as many years as possible but to find a way toward financial independence if not early retirement.[6] Daily news reports lament the imminent collapse of government-subsidized retirement benefits such as Social Security. This shift in long-term planning has led to a major realignment of much economic thinking, from creating a "sharing economy" (such as cars and bikes for hire services), to repeated job-hopping as a method of leveraging higher salaries, to measuring success (early retirement over climbing to the corporate top), to, most important for us, education. Prudent spending is a habit, like good nutrition, that allows people to resist media messages to splurge "just this once" (and then again and again . . .), so the earlier one instills good money management habits, the healthier the person's finances.[7]

See **Lesson 8I—Now or Later?**

See **Lesson 8J—Return to the Scene of the Fun**

See **Lesson 8K—Remorse Code**

CHAPTER 8 ACCOMPANYING LESSONS

Lesson 8A—3N1

Key Concepts
   Children as three-part market participants
Special Materials/Media
   Tally sheet
Intro Questions/Thoughts for Students

- How often (times per week) do you buy things with your own money?
- How often do you ask your parents to buy you something?
- How often do your parents buy you something (like cereal) because you have asked for it before?
- Is there anything you like now that you are pretty sure you will keep buying when you are an adult?

Activity

Children are to fill out the chart below (table 8.1).

Table 8.1.

Things I buy for myself	Brands of the things I buy for myself	Things I ask my parents to buy or that they buy because I have asked for them before	Brands of the things my parents buy for me	Things I use now that I will use when I am an adult	Brands of the things I will buy as an adult
1		1		1	
2		2		2	
3		3		3	

Follow-up Questions/Discussions

- Were any groups easier to fill in three items (or more!) than others?

- Were any groups easier to list brands for than others?
- If you totaled up the cost of each group, which do you think costs the most?
- If you showed the list to your parents, do you think they would be surprised by any of it?

Social Questions for Students

- When is it OK to ask your parents to buy you something, and when is it too much? When does asking become pestering or nagging?
- If someone selling something says, "Try it once," but their plan is to get you to buy a lot, is that OK?

Lesson 8B—It's a Family Affair

Key Concepts
   Children in market, appeal to children and parents
Special Materials/Media
   Access to board game boxes, either online or a visit to a store
Intro Questions/Thoughts for Students

- What is a favorite board or family game you play or have played with other members of your family?
- It's hard to see a complete board game before buying, so how can you know if it is fun? Many times, you learned of a game from a friend, but what about new games or ones you haven't heard of before?
- Do you ever look at the game boxes to get an idea of the games inside? Do you look with your parents, by yourself, or both?

Activity

Students are to look at board game boxes, ether in a store or online. Specifically, they should look for "family-style" games that show the whole family playing and think about: How does the family look?

Follow-up Questions/Discussions

- Do the families look the same way as when your family plays? How is it similar, and how is it different? Do they show the entire family, or just some?
- Do you see families that you think look like your family?
- How are the adults on the boxes participating? Are they playing or cheering? Do they do that in your family?

- How do the ads or board game designs use color or other devices to imply fun? For example, an ad may show the game at an angle or pieces "flying" to imply action.
- Do you ever see anyone unhappy in a game? Look particularly for ads when people lose, for example the timer runs out or a player is sent back to start. Other than the "Oh, no!" head tilt back, do you see real sadness? Why is that?
- Do you think the game boxes are designed to sell to the kids, the parents, or both?

Social Questions for Students

- Have you ever bought or began an activity that you thought would be fun for everyone, but then it just wasn't? Have your parents ever asked you to do something they thought you would enjoy, but you didn't? What did you do? What could you do if that happens? Act out a skit where that happens.

Lesson 8C—Playing Dumb

Key Concepts
    Children's advertising as undermining parental/teacher authority
Special Materials/Media
    Access to children's TV shows or ads toward children
Intro Questions/Thoughts for Students

- If you have a problem, who are the people you must trust for good advice? Your parents? Your teachers?
- What things are your parents and teachers good at giving advice about? What things are your parents and teachers maybe not as good as others at giving advice about?

Activity

Students brainstorm or look for TV shows, movies, or ads that show parents and teachers as clueless or even wrong about life, or where the child is smarter than his or her parents or teachers.

- What is the issue or topic that the parent or teacher is wrong about? Is it something that parents or teachers should know about?
- Does the cluelessness of the adults put the child in danger?
- How does the child deal with the lack of help/support from the adults?

Follow-up Questions/Discussions

- Was there a consistent type of problem that the adults were clueless about? Is it true in your real life, that adults you know are clueless about that topic?
- If you keep getting the message "Don't listen to adults; they don't know," do you think it can affect you, like listening to them about other things in real life? It's fun to solve your own problems, but are there times or problems where you should listen to the adults?
- Why would someone send you a message to not listen to the adults or that adults really don't know?[8]

Social Questions for Students

- How is being a kid today like it was when your parents or teachers were kids, so that they can share their experience as advice, and how do you think it is different?
- What is the difference between being smart and being wise? Can a young or inexperienced person be wise?

Lesson 8D — About Face

Key Concepts
  Marketing to children, cultural impression of children
Special Materials/Media
  Access to Internet to either put together slideshow (such as with PowerPoint) or to print pictures
Intro Questions/Thoughts for Students

- Who are the most important people in America? Who are the most well-known? What is the difference? How much do they overlap?
- How many professional athletes from your hometown or state can you name? TV or film stars? How about scientists or even Nobel Laureates?

Activity

The teacher should create a list of well-recognized and important people. It can include people from government (like the president), sports, and entertainment and a couple of noteworthy scientists or local heroes. Also include some famous historical characters (Abraham Lincoln, Martin Luther King) and some fictional characters elementary kids might know (Iron Man, Wonder Woman). Finally, include some marketing spokespeople, such as Ronald McDonald or Flo (the Progressive Insurance salesperson). Get the list down to ten and then put together a compilation of pictures of each of the ten (without their names on the pic).

The teacher should now survey the students by showing each picture and seeing how many are identified successfully. Use a point system, such as two points for their name, one point for showing knowledge of who the person is but not knowing the name (saying Martin Luther King is "the 'I Have a Dream' man"), and zero for not knowing. Give no hints or help.

Tally up the answers to see who is known best.

Follow-up Questions/Discussions

- Are the best-known people generally celebrities, marketing spokespeople, or people who have done something for the community otherwise (like scientists)?
- Do you think the people who do the most for us should be the most well-known? The nicest? The richest?
- If scientists and others who do a lot for society, but don't really entertain us, are less well-known, what does this say about us? How can we know more about them?

Social Questions for Students

- Who are the most well-known people at your school? Is there a good balance between personalities and types, such as academic kids, athletes, and artists in terms of notoriety? If you could adjust who is recognized (such as in the school's newspaper, in announcements, or on its web page), how would you do it?

Lesson 8E—Political Stick Figures

Key Concepts
   Children as impressionable to social political messaging
Special Materials/Media
   Teacher access to computer to copy pics of political figures
Intro Questions/Thoughts for Students

- We think of "selling" as trying to get people to buy stuff, but do we also "buy" things like how we feel about others? If someone tells you that you should like or not like someone, are they "selling" it to you (or giving it away for free)?

Activity

The teacher should print off a list of pictures of political figures, including local and national. For each one, the student should indicate like, don't like, or don't know them. Then the children should take a copy of the pics home and ask their parents to do the same. The children bring the parents' responses back and compare them with their own to see how many match.

Follow-up Questions/Discussions

- Did more than half match? For how many students was that true?
- Beyond just like or dislike, were there any that were *strong* like or dislike, especially as matched the parents?
- As you are too young to vote, how did you learn about these people or learn to like or dislike them? Did your parents specifically tell you to like or dislike them, or did you just pick it up?
- When you turn eighteen, you will be allowed to vote, but do you think your vote, or at least opinion, is already being shaped? Do you think it is being done intentionally?

Social Questions for Students

- Your parents aren't secretly trying to make you think one way or another, but is it OK for someone to intentionally try to get you to like or dislike someone? Should they let you decide for yourself? Is it OK for them to give you their opinion of the person, especially if they know more about the person or the topic?
- Is there a difference between liking or disliking a person and disagreeing with their opinion? Can you disagree with someone but still like or respect them?
- What is the difference between telling someone, "You are wrong," and telling them, "You are a bad person"?

Lesson 8F—Drawing a Conclusion

Key Concepts
    Marketing to children, cultural impression of children
Special Materials/Media
    Markers/crayons/colored pencils, paper
Intro Questions/Thoughts for Students

- What does it mean to "consume" something? What is a "consumer" in terms of shopping? Why do you think they are called "consumers"?

- Do you remember the first thing you bought for yourself? How old were you? What was it?

Activity

This is a modified version of an actual study done by children's marketers to analyze market penetration. Ask your students to close their eyes and imagine "shopping." Give the children a minute to sit in silence and picture whatever they see, and then have the students draw what they pictured as best they can. Reassure them it doesn't matter if the drawings are good or bad, as they will get a chance to explain their drawing. IMPORTANT: No clues or nudges should be given. If a student says, "Can I draw _____?" tell them to draw whatever they think of with "shopping," that there is no right or wrong.

As the students finish, they should be interviewed about what they drew. You may point and ask, "What is this?" or "Why is that there?" but do not suggest anything, such as asking, "Is that a Target logo?"

Analyze the results with the follow-up questions as tabulating guides.

Follow-up Questions/Discussions

- What are the children's most common type of store (clothing, toys, food, online)?
- Are there any particular shopping centers, malls, or particular stores (by name) depicted? How do you think the child came to know that specific place or name?
- Any particular brands named? Why do you think that brand name became known?
- How often did the child portray themselves (or a child in general)? Is the child happy/sad about shopping?
- How are adults, such as parents or store personnel, depicted?
- How often do the children show any awareness of money or cost in the ad, such as a sale price, a dollar sign, price tags, a cash register, or even the words "on sale"?
- Any trends in special fascinations for children, such as shopping carts, escalators, shopping bags, etc.?
- How much is online shopping portrayed?

Social Questions for Students

- For you, is shopping more just a method to get what you need/want, or is it a fun experience on its own, a social activity? Are there patterns among

your peers as to who sees it one way or the other? Are those attitudes learned or taught?
- For all of the above, are there any general differences between boys and girls? One study found that boys saw shopping more as a chore or way to get what you really wanted while girls saw shopping more as a pleasurable social experience by itself. If you found that, why do you think there is that difference? Are boys and girls taught this difference?

Lesson 8G — Little Big Things

Key Concepts
  Children as future consumers
Special Materials/Media
  None
Intro Questions/Thoughts for Students

- What are brand names of cars you know? You are too young to buy these things, so how do you know about them already?
- Do you have any "mini" or "just for you" versions of products mainly used by older people, like cars or makeup?

Activity

Kids look at home (or on the Internet) for "kid-size" versions of adult products, from food (including kid's meals) to toys to everyday products. If they can, each should bring in or write about one to present about the product and specific brand.

Follow-up Questions/Discussions

- Why do these companies have a kid-size product, especially if kids don't have a lot of money? Are they hoping for something to happen in the future?
- If you know of a brand name, it can become familiar to you. Do you think that gives it an advantage when you have to choose a brand on your own? Some product names, like Kleenex or escalator, started off as only applying to one company's product, but then it became the name people use for all of them!
- Are there any products that should not be allowed to make a kids' version? Cigarette companies used to make "candy cigarettes" for kids, but they were made to stop. What about a sweet drink made by a beer company? What about unhealthy food?

Social Questions for Students

- It's hard to know when you are too young to try something, so how can you know? Can you ask someone? If so, whom?
- Sometimes there are too many choices, so we pick the one we know or have heard of. What is the good or bad of choosing things that way?

Lesson 8H — Breaking Good

Key Concepts
  Getting children to associate childhood centrics (belonging, fun) with a particular product
Special Materials/Media
  None
Intro Questions/Thoughts for Students

- If a Martian came to Earth and asked you to define "fun," what would you say? What activities would you include? If those activities involve a product, what brands would you include?
- We get used to things, so we like to have them around. Are there any products or brands you "can't live without"? Anything that you would be "miserable" without?

Activity

Students think of one to two products (or even better, brands) that they feel make their life fun or that the student thinks they "can't live without." Put everyone's name on a chart and list their product/brand. The students brainstorm alternatives if that product or brand suddenly disappeared. What could they use instead? Students then try to go a week without their preferred brand, using the alternatives instead and marking a hash on the chart every day they do without.

  Afterward, the students present on what they did as a "work-around" and what life was like.

Follow-up Questions/Discussions

- Did you find you could still have fun or quality of life without the product? What does that tell you?
- In fact, many people live happily without most of the things we feel we have to have (or are told we have to have to be happy). What does that tell you about the message that you "must" have something? Why do you

think people (like advertisers) tell you that you "must have" or "need" something?
- Things we have are called "possessions" because we own or "possess" them, but as often stated, we need the thing more than the thing needs us! Some say the less things we "need," the freer we are. Do you agree?

Social Questions for Students

- Here you found a "work-around" (alternative plan) to not having something you want. Can you figure out work-arounds for other times you don't have what you want or need, like knowing the homework assignment because you missed school?

Lesson 8I — Now or Later?

Key Concepts
   Delayed gratification, **investment**
Special Materials/Media
   None
Intro Questions/Thoughts for Students

- Would you rather have a dollar now or a dollar tomorrow? A dollar now or $1.01 tomorrow? A dollar now or five dollars tomorrow? What is your thinking in deciding this?
- Why is it hard to wait for things, even if we know we will get more later by waiting?

Activity

The teacher says the class will be given a chance to "invest" in activity time for the next day. For every minute the class stays quiet (or works hard), they will be given two minutes of free time (or a fun activity) tomorrow. If anyone talks or makes a noise (or gets off task), they have stopped investing (or even spent) the class investment. The teacher can do this up to a maximum amount of time (such as enjoying the quiet).

Follow-up Questions/Discussions

- Was it hard not to "spend" the time and make noise? Why?
- Was it harder for some than others?
- When a person puts away something (or puts into something) so they can get more later, it's called "investing." There are many ways people do this with money (put money into a bank or business, for example, and later get

it back with what is called "interest" or extra money).[9] Ask your parents what investments they have, both for the family and maybe even for you.
- In this simulation, you did not invest money. You invested your effort (to remain quiet) and your time. What other things do you invest effort and time to get back more later? Practicing for a sport or activity? Learning in school?

Social Questions for Students

- One of the biggest investments we can all make is in other people. Being nice, helpful, and a friend takes time and effort, but the payback can be huge (think of *everyone* investing in that). What can you do to invest in your community to make it a better place?

Lesson 8J—Return to the Scene of the Fun

Key Concepts
   Return on investment, investment
Special Materials/Media
   None
Intro Questions/Thoughts for Students

Think of three kinds of toys, games, clothes, or other possessions you have:

- one you have used a lot,
- one you have used off and on, and
- one you have not used a lot or in a long time.

If you can, estimate (or ask your parents) how much each item costs.

Activity

For each of the three types of products, students should try to guess not only the cost but how often they used it (older students can even guess total hours/minutes used). Comparing the cost to how much they used/enjoyed it, they should decide if it was a good use of their money (older students can divide the time used by the cost; younger students can rate it 1–10). If it was a good buy (lots of enjoyment), then it was a good return on investment. If it was a bad buy (low enjoyment), they might think of something else they could have done with the money that would have been a better investment.

Follow-up Questions/Discussions

- We tend to think of things as expensive or cheap, but it depends on how much benefit (good use) we get out of it. A car costs more than cheese, but if you figure it out by the price per pound, the car is cheaper (and it's hard to get to school on a block of cheese!).
- Sometimes the return on investment trickles in but over time can be huge! No one can name a sport (outside gymnastics) that actually requires doing a sit-up in competition, but doing those over and over again helps make one strong for other moves. Is the same true for what you learn in school?

Social Questions for Students

- Think of a time when someone was nice to you. You still like that memory, so that is a great return on investment for that one moment they were nice. Is there ever a bad return on investment to being nice to people?

Lesson 8K—Remorse Code

Key Concepts
   Spending and regret, **buyer's remorse**, investment
Special Materials/Media
   Access to Internet (inflation calculator)
Intro Questions/Thoughts for Students

- Is there anything in your room that you wish, looking back, you had not spent money on? A shirt that is no longer "cool"? A game or toy that was not as much fun as you thought it would be? Something that broke too quickly?

Activity

Students should make a list of things in their room that they now wish they would rather have the money for. They should fill out the three left columns of the chart (table 8.2).

After they come in with their list, the teacher can help them figure out what that money would be today.[10]

Table 8.2.

Item	When obtained	Approximate cost	Value now

Follow-up Questions/Discussions

- What kinds of things could you use that money for today? Looking back, would you rather have had the things or the money (plus interest) now?
- We can't take back a decision from a couple of years ago, but how can we learn from this? For future purchases, can we ask ourselves if, in two to three years, we will like that we spent the money? Maybe something better will come along?
- We also tend to ask what else we could have bought for ourselves, but are there other things we could do with it, like give it to a charity?

Social Questions for Students

- Are there any things you did to someone in the past that, looking back, you wish you had not? It's too late to undo it, but is it ever too late to say you are sorry?

NOTES

1. Other than that it's a requirement of Texas citizenship to work it into all conversations with non-Texans.
2. James U. McNeal, *Kids as Customers: A Handbook of Marketing to Children* (New York: Lexington Books, 1992), 14–17.
3. See, for example, Holly K. M. Henry and Dina L. G. Borzekowski. *The Nag Factor: How Do Children Convince Their Parents to Buy Unhealthy Foods?* Johns Hopkins University Bloomberg School of Public Health, August 11, 2011, https://www.jhsph.edu/news/news-releases/2011/borzekowski-nag-factor.html. It's also referred to as "pester power."
4. Gary Ruskin, "Why They Whine: How Corporations Prey on Our Children," Mothering Magazine, July 1, 2003, http://www.mothering.com/10-0-0/html/10-3-0/10-3-whine97.shtml.
5. See, for example, the issue of inculcating poor financial habits (even gambling) through video games, as discussed at https://parentology.com/prince-harry-fortnite-gaming-addictive/.
6. Called the FIRE (Financial Independence, Early Retirement) movement. We do not note this increasing desire to retire early in a negative way, as some critics of Millennials have. Rather, we applaud their goal if those who desire it can truly achieve it.
7. We realize we are advocating here with financial literacy yet another insertion into your already packed curriculum. A teacher's patience is never more tested than when a person suggests or even insists that a subject important to them "should be worked into your lessons." The teacher smiles and thanks the person for the suggestion, suppressing all desire to sarcastically say, "Oh my gosh, THANK YOU! You know, I had about two weeks where the kids just sat around doing nothing, and I was hoping someone would come in and fill that gap for me!"

One of us had a habit of rebuffing all administration calls for curriculum additions with "Great! Get back to me with exactly what I take out of my curriculum to make room and I'll consider it." Feel free to write us the same. In addition to our lessons, there are ever-growing resources for teachers who desire to find out more about financial literacy, including NGPF (Nest Gen Personal Finance), at https://www.ngpf.org/.

8. Ironically, it's adult advertisers that are sending the message not to listen to adults, of course!

9. We won't go into the details that the institution invested in is technically paying the investor for borrowing the money.

10. There are several ways to do this. First, the teacher can decide if the student should use the actual number of years ago each item was bought or just use an average number of years. Second, the teacher can calculate the "lost investment" using an investment calculator (http://www.moneychimp.com/features/simple_interest_calculator.htm), using 10 percent, or just figuring out what that money spent back then would be worth today (https://www.usinflationcalculator.com/). Or the teacher can skip all this and just use the flat amount spent.

Chapter Nine

Media Literacy, Relativity, and Persuasion

There is an old joke (which usually means it's no longer funny) in Boy Scouting:

Question: How do you tell a Boy Scout?

Answer: In a calm, soothing voice so as not to startle the Boy Scout before telling him what you want to say!

Slightly more profound (though certainly not as grandpa knee-slapping humorous), philosopher and early pioneer of media literacy Marshall McLuhan famously said that "the medium is the message," meaning that the way a message is conveyed is just as important and has just as much an effect on listeners as the content of the message itself.[1] In both the joke and McLuhan's statement, the idea is that the modality of how a message is conveyed is as much a part of the persuasion as the merits of the message itself. To put it another way, we think of ourselves as stationary, catching messages as they come to us and then deciding for ourselves if the message has merit and therefore should be embraced.

In economics, this same idea is often summed up by the notion of **consumer sovereignty**, that the consumer of goods (or information)[2] has the last and ultimate control of what is produced or is successful in the market. In both cases, however, it is a question of relativity; the consumer may think they are stationary, but they have been actually brought closer to the message by the message delivery techniques, so that they are quicker to take it in and more receptive to inculcating the core message into their belief system.

Whether one puts this relativism in terms of media literacy, Einsteinian metaphors about two moving trains, or even Michel de Montaigne's sixteenth-century question "When I am playing with my cat, how do I know she is not playing with me?" consumers of information need to be aware of how they are being primed for the message, as well as how the message is being primed for them.

This is especially true for children, who are being messaged by seasoned adults with abstract thought, communication tricks, and money that can be used to persuade the child to believe just about *anything*. Consider how many children might fall for a line like, "For that dirty, wadded-up old dollar bill in your pocket, I'll give you three new shiny quarters that you can flip and do tricks with!"[3]

Empathy develops at a very young age—as young as two years old—and while it remains a valuable window through which we can see, understand, and connect with others, that window is also a portal into our souls by those who would nudge us to respond favorably to their own messaging ends using humor, love, and other emotional touchpoints to make us more receptive before the message is even heard.[4]

Ivan Pavlov was the famous Russian researcher who showed that if something neutral, like ringing a bell, was activated at the same time as something good—feeding his dogs—the dogs came to link the two and have positive reactions to the bell alone. His dogs would salivate in anticipation when they heard the ringing of the bell. Can such conditioning also happen with ads, where one's positive feelings toward a good ad, over time, become linked to the product itself?

In a less direct method, sometimes bringers of bad (or a least unwelcomed) information "butter up" the information receiver by first delivering good news or amusing them, or by laying out a general persuasive argument so that the receiver is in a more congenial or receptive mood once the unwelcomed bit comes at the end. Even Thomas Jefferson remembered his media literacy and persuasion lessons by laying out his arguments from general to more specific in his famous break-up letter to King George, only actually declaring America's independence in the last paragraph.

See Lesson 9A—In the Mood

Even as we arrive at the spot to hear and experience the information or point of view of the messenger, we arrive with baggage in hand, that baggage being our own biases that become more entrenched when confirmed but resistant if challenged or countered. Interestingly, the word stereotype comes from the idea of mass printing, where a plate is used to print the same thing over and over again (like a picture reproduction). And yes, elementary children already have baggage, or at least tote-bag copies of their parents' baggage.[5]

See **Lesson 9B—Martian Chronicles**

For children just starting on the information path, they look for an extending path to follow: how should they carry on with the new information just handed to them?[6] Do they believe it? Do they weigh the message with rational thinking or gut feeling? They are supposed to go somewhere or do something because of the message, but where and what?

Like any new arrival to a new place, they look for signs to guide them, and information peddlers are more than happy to point the way. Contained in the messages are focus nudges to guide them but that can make child consumers only consider what the messengers allude to rather than seeing all the sites. This creates a potential problem of children being focus-nudged into assumptions, presumptions, and overgeneralizations, especially when the messenger, knowingly or unknowingly, curates the message to give an imbalanced overview or slant.

One of us does a quick demonstration for classes by standing at the front of the room and asking students to intensely focus on his finger that is held up. After thirty seconds, the teacher asks the class if, while they looked at his finger, they saw the second hand of the clock ticking away about three feet above the finger. Most of the class says they did not, but the teacher then reminds them that the laws of physics did not change; light continued to refract off the second hand and into their eyes, the students just chose to ignore those light signals because the teacher instructed them to! In media terms, we see this in services that provide summation (like thirty-minute news programs) or "headline" news; we focus on the "top stories" because we are told they are the top stories, even if one station's top story is a potential war on the other side of the world while another's is about a local boy trapped in a well. Tell a child that something, practically *anything*, is important, and they will believe you and focus on it.

See **Lesson 9C—Crime Scene**

See **Lesson 9D—Seeing in Two Dimensions**

Whether a message is skewed intentionally or unintentionally, message receivers need to be aware of such nudges so that they can countersteer or at least begin to be aware that their attention is being pulled a certain way by the words, pictures, and other stimuli that accompany the message. To be clear, there really is no such thing as an unbiased, nonslanted message. There are so many facts regarding any particular issue that as soon as a messenger decides fact A is worth relaying in detail, fact B should be summarized, or fact C should be left out, they have curated the transferal of information and opened the door to possible inaccuracies, misdepictions, and misunderstanding.

Most of this may be too complex and sophisticated for some children, but as teachers know, if one can get a child one time to say, "AHA! I see what you did there!" you have opened the door to a second, third, and then a floodgate of empowerment for the child to take control of message transferal and reception.

As discussed before, children like rules that are reasonable but clear-cut with few exceptions. It makes the complex world an easier place to navigate. This can, however, lead to children falling prey to a common **fallacy** called a hasty generalization,[7] where a person assumes everyone or everything of a group is like a very (too) small sample. As long as we are on guard and look for such possibilities, however, we are still the better for being exposed to and exchanging divergent information and perspectives. It's like human interaction: mixing with people increases your risk of catching a cold, but as long as we take precautions, life is better shared with others than alone in an antiseptic cell.

See **Lesson 9E—Mountain of Information**

See **Lesson 9F—Aligning Words and Actions**

If one or two words can nudge us into thinking a certain way, imagine what pictures can do, given that they are purportedly worth one thousand words (and that's for simple pictures at the old exchange rates). Because we rarely consciously say, "Look at that," but instead take in most visuals passively, it's important to teach children to be aware of any preset filters on their radar. Even what's not center to our viewing but merely "background" can add meaning to what we are focused on.

See **Lesson 9G—Feeling in the Pink, or Are You Blue?**

See **Lesson 9H—No Problem**

When we see two things side by side, we can't help but compare and contrast them. This is called juxtaposition, and it can be done verbally ("Whereas . . . ") or pictorially with "before" and "after" pictures. When a messenger sets up a picture (or anything in it, such as colors) to make you think a certain way, this is called **implied messaging**. It persuades us through our "gut" response (**visceral processing**) rather than our mental (rational) processing.

Even being aware of our own visual presumptions is not enough, as we then have to consider how the messenger's presumptions and visual interpretations seep into our own seemingly internal, independent valuation. Search engines like Google are not all-knowing entities that always give the "right" answer, but use algorithms, complex sets of coded rules based on other (and your) human assumptions and slants, to decide what you most likely want in your latest Internet search.

See **Lesson 9I—Drawn In**

Finally, while we are predisposed to first and perhaps primarily take in the world by our eyes, our ears are likewise taking in the world (and never getting a break at night, like our eyes do). Maybe because they're on the sides of our head and we don't think about them (until cold weather hits), we associate certain sounds with perceptions, and ancient media as far back as radio have been masters at giving us sounds (like a creaky door or a car horn changing pitch as it seems to pass) and letting us draw the accompanying pictorial conclusions.

See **Lesson 9J—Oh, What a Knight!**

See **Lesson 9K—Noisy Theater of the Mind**

CHAPTER 9 ACCOMPANYING LESSONS

Lesson 9A—In the Mood

Key Concepts
    Emotionally affecting a message receiver prior to the message
Special Materials/Media
    Stories of different genres (scary, comedy, adventure) or movies of different genres
Intro Questions/Thoughts for Students

- What are the different kinds of stories or movies (suspense, comedy, adventure)?
- Does it help to get into a story if you are in the right "frame of mind"? Does it make you more open to accept what is going on if you are looking for funny or scary?

Activity

Part 1—The teacher reads the opening paragraph of stories from different genres. The class tries to guess the "mood" or genre of the story. The teacher can also follow up by saying she is going to read the opening of a very scary story, but then read the opening of a funny story to see if the students say, "That's not right!"

Part 2—The teacher can repeat this with the opening music (overture) to movies of different genres (rom-com, thriller, etc.) and see if the students can guess what kind of movie it will be.

Follow-up Questions/Discussions

- Why do books and movies do this? Even for stories and movies with twists, they still generally like to set the mood.
- If you think a story is one way (comedy), but it goes another (scary), does it throw you "off" so you are not as into the story?
- Advertisements try to do this as well. An ad for a drink might want you to think about being thirsty before they show you the drink or laughing before they tell you about a product. Why do they do this?

Social Questions for Students

- Do you ever try to get someone in a certain mood before you tell them something? Do you ever say, "This is serious," or get your parents in a good mood before you ask their permission?

Lesson 9B—Martian Chronicles

Key Concepts
Stereotypes in media, feedback loop (self-validation) of expectations and behaviors, **confirmation bias**
Special Materials/Media
Access to media
Intro Questions/Thoughts for Students

- How much of what we think about others is based on media images telling us what we should be? When media portray particular groups, like kids or soccer players, do they show a wide variety of possibilities, or do they tend to show a few certain stereotypes? How can we tell when we are seeing a stereotype?[8]
- Once you have an idea about something, do you generally assume all such things are like that? What is an example of a thing or place you tried once and then assumed it was always like that?
- Have you ever assumed someone likes or doesn't like something, or does or does not do an activity, based on how they look (like assuming a tall person plays basketball)?

Activity

You are a Martian sent as a spy to investigate and report back on Earth (and particularly American) culture. You know nothing of Earth, but figure you can learn about Earthlings' ways by monitoring their media.

Watch various media, and look for general observations to report back to your leader about different groups, such as:

- men and women, especially those with particular features (such as blondes or wearing glasses);
- people from particular regions of the world (such as the Middle East) or the United States (such as the South or Hollywood);
- people of particular ages, races, socioeconomic status, or roles (such as parents); and
- activities, such as high school classes or spring break.

Remember, you know nothing beforehand, so everything you learn about this group/activity is from its general portrayal in media. A human wearing sunglasses inside might indicate humans are very light sensitive (which must be typical because no one is telling him not to do so).

Follow-up Questions/Discussions

- You already know something about most of the types of people you saw, so you can often tell when a person is not a good representative of a group. But what about types of people you don't know a lot about? Do you think you might have a skewed view of them like the Martian would?
- When you hear of something "everyone is doing," have you ever then joined in, which ultimately makes the original statement true (even if it wasn't originally)? This is called a feedback loop. What are the positives and negatives of such a phenomenon?
- If our primary way for knowing about people is based on stereotypes, we might think of that stereotype and look to confirm it, reinforcing our belief (and labeling those that don't fit the stereotype as "weird" or "abnormal"). It's like when once a person is known as clumsy, we only notice him when he trips, never when he makes a brilliant leaping move.

Social Questions for Students

- What things do people assume about you because you identify as belonging to a certain group? What might be a stereotype you assume about other groups?

- Have you ever acted a certain way or expressed an opinion because people expected you to more than that you really wanted to?
- Do people think of you in a certain way (such as clumsy) that you think is untrue or unfair?

Lesson 9C — Crime Scene

Key Concepts
   Subjective point of view in understanding something
Special Materials/Media
   A friend the students don't know, suspect identification sheet
Intro Questions/Thoughts for Students

- What does it mean to be a witness to something?

NOTE: As this exercise relies on surprise, no more introductory questions should be asked.

Activity

As the teacher is talking with the class, a "stranger" should interrupt and ask where the gym/cafeteria is located. Depending on the class setup, the teacher should walk away from his desk to point it out, at which point the stranger grabs something off the desk (maybe the teacher's wallet or a knickknack), says, "I've got it now!" and runs out. The teacher yells something (like "Drop it, you thief!") and runs after the stranger.

Immediately (so as to minimize upset), have the teacher return and say that was a demonstration, but the class just witnessed a "crime." The class is now asked by the police to fill out a witness report in which they must describe what exactly happened in all details, what was said and done (in exact order), and, most of all, what the thief looked like, including

- approximate height and weight,
- distinguishing hair/marks, and
- clothing (if you can, have the thief wear a patterned shirt or one with a logo and one odd thing like mismatched shoes or a rose in his/her hair).

Afterward, the class can compare and see who got what right or was most complete. The class loves to see the thief after they fill out their report; the thief will love the descriptions of him or her!

Follow-up Questions/Discussions

- Were the "reports" very different?
- Some people seem better to ID height and weight, others clothes. Why is that?
- Most of all, how could so many people seeing the exact same thing be so different? What does this tell you about needing multiple viewpoints?

Social Questions for Students

- We tend to decide if we like someone or something on our own, but does it help to get different perspectives from different people? Why?
- Can there be too many opinions? When should you just trust your own opinion?

Lesson 9D—Seeing in Two Dimensions

Key Concepts
    Fact vs. opinion (**editorial**) in news
Special Materials/Media
    Newspaper or printable online news source, two colors of highlighter
Intro Questions/Thoughts for Students

- What is the difference between a fact and an opinion? When people say they are "just giving us the facts," are they always? Can you tell when an opinion is portrayed as a fact?
- What is an editorial? Why are they usually separated from news articles?

Activity

Students should locate the op-ed page of a newspaper and read editorials (or columns by professionals on news sites). Break down the writer's claims by highlighting the *facts* he or she uses in one color and their *opinions* in another color. Compare to other students' evaluations of the same piece. If one student marked something as a fact and another student marked it as opinion, discuss why each of you thought that.

   As follow-up, students should find an editorial that gives an opinion on the same issue but from the other side and do the same thing. Finally, circle any facts mentioned in one piece but not the other.

   To make it simpler, students can also do this with restaurant reviews, separating facts ("The chicken costs $10") from opinion ("The chicken was delicious!").

Follow-up Questions/Discussions

- If two people arguing use different facts, can we get a clear picture by one source? Can you have "your facts" and "my facts" or must all facts be considered by everyone to get the whole picture?
- Were there any contradictory facts? How can we resolve this?
- Would a third opinion help? Why or why not?
- What is the danger of thinking an opinion is a fact?

Social Questions for Students

- We sometimes see the world as black or white, as "You either agree and are with me or disagree and are against me." When is this true/false way of looking at things helpful, and when is it counterproductive?
- When is compromise good, and when is it important to stand firm?

Lesson 9E — Mountain of Information

Key Concepts
    Labels affecting perception, confirmation bias
Special Materials/Media
    Picture of a mountain
Intro Questions/Thoughts for Students

- Have you ever thought that something or someone was a certain way, only to find out later it was different (or seen differently by other people)?
- Are there things that you haven't yet tried but you already know whether or not you would like them? How do you know that? Are there people you have never met but you already hear they are nice or mean (like the teachers you will have next year)?
- What is a **preconception**?

Activity

The class is divided into four groups. Each is shown (secretly) the same picture of a mountain, but each group's picture has a different caption:

- Mountain of Doom
- Sugar Sweet Mountain
- Mountain of Peace
- Adventure Mountain

Each group then makes up a story about the mountain and an event that happens on it, including adjectives that describe the mountain and how it looks. Bonus if they can come up with music that would be played in the background to the picture!

Reveal the picture and ask which group had this picture. Read the different stories aloud.

Follow-up Questions/Discussions

- How do the stories and adjectives about the mountain differ? Does the mountain look different as you read the different stories? Is it hard to see the mountain in a new way?
- When you hear someone has a title or job (doctor, scientist, teacher), do you assume things about them before you have met them? Is this fair?

Social Questions for Students

- Do you ever judge people by what you are told about them before actually getting to know them? What are the first images you get in your mind of a kid who is a "jock," a "social person," or a "religious person"?
- Can you think of a situation where you began by having one perception but then it changed? Why did you have that first perception, and why did it change?

Lesson 9F — Aligning Words and Actions

Key Concepts
   Aligning actions and words, implication
Special Materials/Media
   None (except space for movement)
Intro Questions/Thoughts for Students

- We think of communication as mainly with words, but how much meaning do we also convey with our physical actions? Aside from nodding "yes" or shaking our head "no," how often do we rely on physical gestures to communicate, and how do we interpret that?

Activity

In groups of three, students come to the front of the room. One of the three steps outside the class (this will be Student 3). Student 1 then reads a slip of paper silently with a message, such as "Do your math homework" or "Would you like to come to my party?" Student 1 gets two minutes to silently act out the message to Student 2. Student 2 is not to say what they think the message is, just receive it. Student 3 then is brought in and Student 2 must again act out the message to Student 3, but this time it is done as charades where Student 3 may guess out loud and Student 2 may confirm responses or guide them. After Student 3 guesses the perceived message (or a time limit is reached), Student 3's perceived message is compared with Student 1's.

An alternate version is to pick an object. Student 1 may only describe it to Student 2 (but cannot use physical movement or name it). Student 2 must then only act out the object or its use without words (or looking at it if the object is in the room) to Student 3.

Follow-up Questions/Discussions

- Were the messages conveyed to Student 3 more often correct or incorrect? What were the hardest things to communicate: verbs, objects, or places? Why do you think that is?
- Besides shaking or nodding our head, what are ways we add meaning to the words we use? Can a body movement (or tone) change the meaning? Try saying, "Yeah, right," with different meaning based on tone and actions.
- If meaning can be distorted by changing actions into words, what about words into other words? Go to Google Translate and type in a famous phrase ("To be or not to be, that is the question" or "The only thing we have to fear is fear itself"). Translate the phrase into another language, translate that translation into a third (preferably non-Western) language,[9] and then translate it back into English. What did you get?

Social Questions for Students

- When you have disagreements, are they over differences of opinion or differences in understanding, such as when your parents say to do something but don't specifically say "now"? How can you tell the difference and avoid misinterpretation?
- Have you ever had in mind what you want to say but couldn't find the words in the moment? What did you do?

Lesson 9G—Feeling in the Pink, or Are You Blue?

Key Concepts
    Color as visual persuasion, implied messaging
Special Materials/Media
    Access to Internet or magazines
Intro Questions/Thoughts for Students

- Do colors mean something or imply certain ideas? What does the color red imply to you by itself? In **context**, when does it mean something good, and when does it mean something bad? Green? Blue? White? Black? Is there an implied "language of color"?
- Does the meaning of color change by culture? What color is associated with marriage in the United States, and what color in China? How did we get to have two colors mean the same thing? Is there logic to what colors mean?

Activity

In groups have students brainstorm associations of the color spectrum (red, orange, yellow, green, blue, indigo, and violet) as well as white, black, and clear (no color) with meanings or imagery. Students should try to think of positive and negative associations or circumstances for each color if they can. Students should then share and make a compiled list.

Students can follow up in two ways. First, make a list of words on a slide presentation or pieces of paper but put some in the "wrong color" (put "grass" in blue and "sky" in green, or "heaven" in red and "hell" in blue) along with other words that are in the "right" colors as determined by the class ("fast" in red). Showing these words to non-classmates (such as friends or parents), do the subjects notice anything (or anything "wrong") about the words?

Alternatively, students can think of types of products (cleaning products, health products, cars, money services, etc.) and think what colors, in their opinion, "should" be associated with that kind of product. Students should then test their hypothesis by observing ads.[10]

Finally, the class can play charades where students have to guess the color "acted out."

Follow-up Questions/Discussions

- If "grass" means the same in any color, how can the color be "wrong"? Is there a second message that is conveyed by color?
- Are colors used not only to convey a message but to affect you or to put you in a mood? Can it be like the way someone might say, "Thank you"? Have the class look up paint companies (such as Glidden or Sherwin-Williams) that describe colors as reflecting certain moods to see if the students agree.
- Is there a difference between the color being "wrong" and "not right"?
- When you pre-guessed colors with a product and then looked for them, did you notice them because you were right or because you were now looking for that color to confirm you were right (confirmation bias)?

Social Questions for Students

- What is your favorite color? Is there something it represents to you? Have students group themselves by favorite color. Does the color mean the same to everyone in a group?
- For you, what are the "colors" of abstract ideas such as friendship, love, or hate? Why?

Lesson 9H — No Problem

Key Concepts
   Background as affecting perception of what we are observing
Special Materials/Media
   Computer to make signs
Intro Questions/Thoughts for Students

- When you look at something, do you just look at it or do you consider where it is and the things around it?

Activity

The teacher should take a picture of a person with a caption of them saying, "No problem." The picture should be superimposed on various backgrounds; however, make one of a beautiful park, one of a house on fire or a volcano erupting, one with a bad guy just behind him, and one at the student's school. The teacher can then either:

- show each as a slide to the class and for each ask the students what the person is thinking when they say, "No problem," or
- divide the class into groups, giving each group a different picture and have them make up a story about the person and why he is saying, "No problem." Each presents.

Follow-up Questions/Discussions

- Each group or photo had the same main subject and statement, but did it seem different by what was in the background? Why?
- Trying to understand something by the surrounding circumstances is called understanding something in context. Can you think of another example?
- Putting things in context is usually helpful, but can it distract us or make us assume the wrong thing? A shiny, healthy apple is just as nutritious if

you see it in a bowl of fruit or surrounded by trash. When can judging something by its surroundings be bad?

Social Questions for Students

- Do you judge people by the things around them, and is that bad? Is it OK to judge someone by where they live, their friends, or their clothes?
- Have you ever been judged by things around you rather than just you? Was that fair? Does it depend on whether you can control if those things are around you?

Lesson 9I—Drawn In

Key Concepts
   Visceral versus rational consideration of messages, pathos versus logos in persuasion
Special Materials/Media
   Access to ads
Intro Questions/Thoughts for Students

- What kinds of decisions do you think through, considering all the facts first in a removed, analytical (rational) approach to deciding, and in which do you use a more quick, emotional, gut (visceral) response? Which is best for deciding where to go to eat? How to invest money? What to buy a friend for a birthday present?
- In making your decision, do others try to nudge you to use more reason or emotion to decide? What clues tell you that the messenger wants you to take your time and think it out using reason or that they want you to make a quick gut decision?

Activity

The teacher should bring in print ads and students decide if the appeal (persuasive technique) is more to the viewer's rational (removed) side or to one's emotional (gut) side. Some clues that might help:

- Does the ad use numbers or graphs that take a while to understand?
- Does the ad make you a removed observer (faraway shot or putting the depicted scene in a frame so as to make clear you are outside) to say, "Be a scientist and think it through," or does the ad try to draw you in (close-up shots or someone in the ad is looking right at you) so that it's saying, "You are here; decide now!"?

- Does the ad depict "emotional tugs" such as a cute animal or a common fear?
- Does the ad offer a logical solution to a problem?

Follow-up Questions/Discussions

- Are some kinds of products more geared to emotion ("Join the fun!") and some more to logic ("It works")? Why is that?
- The use of emotion to persuade (pathos) and the use of facts, logic, or reasoning (logos) are separate techniques, but do you often use both to decide something? How so?[11]
- Movie posters often have the main actors looking right at the viewer; why do you think that is?
- Do you see messaging that uses pathos and logos at school or at home?

Social Questions for Students

- Is it OK to use someone's fear of something to persuade them? How about the fear of having no friends if they don't spend a lot of money to look good? How about the fear of harm if they use drugs or alcohol?

Lesson 9J—Oh, What a Knight!

Key Concepts
   Effect of auditory cues on perception
Special Materials/Media
   Picture of a knight (can be obtained from the Internet), three to four theme songs (also obtained from the Internet)
Intro Questions/Thoughts for Students

- Stop the class and be silent for a minute. What did you hear? Whatever you are hearing, do you hear that when it is not silent? The answer is most probably yes (the sound waves are still vibrating against your ear drum), but you just don't notice it.
- How much does sound affect how we perceive things? How does music (such as a villain's theme song that plays whenever he enters)[12] affect what we think about a movie character or what we anticipate will happen?

Activity

Divide the students into four groups. Tell each they will write a story based on a picture and accompanying music. Each group should work away from the others and not hear or look at the other groups' materials. Each group is then given (secretly) the *same* picture of a knight or castle.

Each group is given a link, however, to four different kinds of background music:

- ominous, scary music;
- heroic, adventure music;
- fun, light-hearted music; or
- romantic music.

When the groups are ready, have them take turns playing the music and reading the story. After all have gone, show that they had the same picture.

Follow-up Questions/Discussions

- Were there differences in how each group saw the picture? Was it hard to adjust to another group's way of seeing the knight?
- Where else is sound used to affect how you see things? In stores, what kind of music do they play (and what mood do they want you to be in)? How about TV shows? Do they use music to affect your mood and how you see things? Compare the opening themes of a comedy, a mystery, and an action show.
- Can other senses such as smell, taste, or touch affect how we perceive things?

Social Questions for Students

- Do you have "go to" music for certain moods? When you are sad, do you prefer sad music that aligns with your mood or happy music to help you not be so sad? What is your "get excited" music?
- If you were a movie character with a set background theme every time you entered a scene, what song or kind of music would it be?

Lesson 9K—Noisy Theater of the Mind

Key Concepts
   Sound as influencing imagery
Special Materials/Media
   Miscellaneous objects to make sound effects
Intro Questions/Thoughts for Students

- Have you ever had an image in your mind of the way something looks but then been disappointed or thrown off when you saw how it really looked (or how someone else portrayed it)?
- Is it easier to use imagination with just hearing something or just seeing something? Why?

Activity

A Foley artist is a person who adds everyday sounds to movies, like moving shoes across crispy cereal to sound like walking on gravel or imitating with their mouth a creaky door opening. Students should be divided into groups with each group preparing to tell other students a fairy tale. The groups should have a narrator, various students taking different voice parts, and some in the group being Foley artists who add sound effects. As an added challenge, the group must stop at some point and do a fifteen- to thirty-second ad for a product related to the story (Pete's porridge, Little Red's riding hoods), complete with slogan and jingle. The groups take turns presenting with the listeners sitting or lying comfortably but with their eyes closed.

Follow-up Questions/Discussions

- Was it hard to come up with ways to imitate sounds? Was it fun? Why?
- Was it hard to not talk or to not make noise when it was your turn to be quiet? Why so?
- For listening, how did the sounds affect your picturing of the story?

Social Questions for Students

- We are often so busy seeing that we miss a lot of interesting sounds. When we focus less on seeing, we appreciate the sounds more, even if for a little while. The same is true for all the activities we do. If we are so busy trying to get the next thing done (or worrying how we will do it), can we miss the fun and good times in the moment? What is a good thing you have in your daily life that you rarely take time to appreciate, like having meals when you want them? What do your parents wish they had appreciated more when they were younger?
- Try walking to class for a day without making noise and just listening. For each walk, what is something new you heard or something you never noticed before?

NOTES

1. For those of you who bought the book looking to immediately dive into pure media lit exercises, thank you for your patience. We believe the nine-chapter wait was worth it!
2. See also discussion at Lesson 6H.
3. In another sideways parent story here, the then-six-year-old son of one of the authors came home frustrated as he had given away a fairly rare card from a popular battle game to another child in exchange for a promise to eventually give him an ultimate secret, all-powerful card the child was "personally developing." It had been over a week, and no all-powerful card had been proffered. Miraculously, however, the two boys remained friends throughout childhood, and upon the duplicitous child's earning an MBA, the son gave him a congratulatory note saying, "Congrats on your MBA. Still waiting for my card!"
4. See Lesson 4G.
5. See chapter 7 about children imitating parents in aspirational views.
6. This remains true throughout one's life as one explores any new line of inquiry.
7. See also Lesson 4F. And yes, we realize the irony of a generalization that discusses the fallacy of generalizations. Do as we say, not as we do!
8. See Lesson 6B about stereotypes.
9. Don't just keep changing the destination language of the original English. You need to put the translated words (such as those just into Spanish) now over to the left side "translate from" box (or hit the reverse arrows) and then pick a third language (such as Thai or Chinese) for the other box, then repeat by translating the third language phrase back into English.
10. This can also be done for certain demographic groups, like boys, girls, young, old, professionals, etc.
11. The third type of persuasion, ethos (appeal by the spokesperson) is addressed in Lesson 4C.
12. Google or use YouTube to find Darth Vader's theme as an example.

Chapter Ten

Telling the Truth

Media literacy and its cousin, consumer economics, seem to be recent arrivals in the field of deconstruction and analysis of communication, but in fact they have been a part of mankind's decoding tools for a very long time. Schools that say, "We need to teach media literacy" are (while correct!) overlooking that every time a language or literature teacher challenges students to find meaning in a passage, *they are engaging in a media literacy exercise*. Every art teacher who challenges his or her students to find or express meaning through nonverbal techniques is part of a media literacy chain that stretches back perhaps forty thousand years to early humans creating and viewing cave paintings.

James Madison, the father of our Constitution, wrote more than 230 years ago as to our national and societal need for diversity of opinion. In Federalist Paper #10, he insisted that a necessary check on tyranny and oppression was nothing less than a diverse body of people with varying opinions. In such a mix, for any idea or point of view to gain the support of a majority of the people, it had to be so good as to win over a wide variety of those different perspectives.

Today, we have achieved a diverse population beyond any Madison could have dreamed of. What we need to do now is learn how to listen to each other, take in all of the varied ways we communicate this diversity of thought, and figure out how to separate and hold onto the good ideas held in common, for the common good. We also need to train our youth to see through the smoke and mirrors, so as to be able to see past the terrible Wizard of Oz to the real man behind the curtain, for who he truly is and what his message means.

Much is being said of late about "fake news" amid worry for how quickly misinformation spreads across social networks. An old adage, at least a hundred years old (and ascribed in various forms to everyone from Jonathan Swift to Mark Twain), is that *a lie can travel halfway around the world while truth is still putting on its shoes.* In today's world of instant media, truth sometimes hasn't even woken up.

Bending the truth. Not giving the full story. Shading. Dissimulating. Falsifying. The prevalence of so many synonyms and euphemisms for lying can make one despair at what humans have done with one of the greatest gifts we have, language and the art of communication. Whether being exhorted to consume tangible goods or intangible ideas, people today are bombarded with prepackaged solutions that promise a better life, but is that better life for the consumer or the purveyor of what's being sold?

Like any tool, the ability to communicate can be used for good or ill will, and so we must teach people, especially our youth, how to recognize improper use and how to defend themselves against harm. As predominantly middle- and high-school teachers in K–12 schools, we, the authors, were often thanked by graduating students for all we had done to prepare them to take on the world. We would have to remind them, however, that education is like a building. All the pretty decorative work is on the top floors, but they are nothing without the solid foundation and first-floor door one passes through every day yet takes for granted. Instilling these skills in students while in elementary school may seem like they are not done in depth, but everything else, including a student's later success in life, rests on it.[1]

See **Lesson 10A—To Tell the Truth**

See **Lesson 10B—Media Begins with ME**

CHAPTER 10 ACCOMPANYING LESSONS

Lesson 10A—To Tell the Truth

Key Concepts
   Detecting who is telling the truth versus who is lying, **tells**
Special Materials/Media
   None
Intro Questions/Thoughts for Students

- How can you tell when someone is telling the truth or not? What clues can you discover in how a person tells a story to judge whether or not you should believe it? What physical signs might you look for?

Activity

This is a variation of the old TV game show *To Tell the Truth*. Three students are taken out into the hall and are asked for some interesting trivia about themselves (such as one met a celebrity at an airport, one won a tournament, or one has an unusual secret hobby). The teacher then brings the three students in before the class and announces that one of the students has an interesting fact and describes it generally ("They met a famous person while on vacation"). The rest of the class then asks questions of the three about the topic (it's best to mandate a rotational response, so question 1 goes to panelist 1, question 2 to panelist 2, question 3 to 3, then back to 1 so all are asked). The panelists must observe these rules:

- The one for whom the story is true may not lie and must always answer truthfully.
- The other two are free to make up stuff, but it must be believable (their job is to try to convince people).

At the end of the questioning (either timed or two to three questions for each questioner), the class votes on which panelist they believe the story is about. The truth teller is then revealed.

Alternatively, this can be done with three teachers as panelists.

Follow-up Questions/Discussions

- How did you choose your questions? Were they more open-ended or yes/no?
- Did the questioners each ask their own questions or did they build off each other (follow-up)? Which is more effective?
- Did anyone ask, "Are you telling the truth?" or "Are you lying?" Was that helpful?
- Aside from answers to questions, what other things did you notice, such as body movement or hesitating in answering, especially for the ones making up the story? These are called tells and are used by many people, from police to poker players, to assess believability.
- Are some people better at faking it than others? Why do you think that is?

Social Questions for Students

- How do we draw the line between exaggerating a story to make it more interesting and outright lying?

- Is lying ever OK? Is there a difference between lying about meeting a famous person and lying about copying someone's homework?

Lesson 10B — Media Begins with ME

Key Concepts
   Overall competency of media literacy
Special Materials/Media
   Computer or posters
Intro Questions/Thoughts for Students

- There are a lot of things "sold" to you in the way of products, but are opinions sold to you as well? Do people try to "sell" themselves by winning you over or getting you to like them?
- When are times you need to present, even "sell" yourself? School interviews? Meeting new friends? Maybe meeting your teacher next year?

Activity

Students are to make a promo skit or even video (one to two minutes) imagining they are making it to introduce themselves to their teacher next year (or for a job, to go into middle school, etc.). We call it *This Is Me*. They are to use at least three of the media literacy techniques discussed throughout this book.

   Each student should first plan their video by choosing up to three aspects of themselves (activities, qualities) that they feel best reflect who they are. They should then think of three ways to promote or "sell" those qualities. It could be by background shot of a soccer field (chapter 9) or a testimonial by their current teacher. They should also think about the kinds of things that would "nudge" someone to "buy" the message (chapter 4) that would promote their coolness (chapter 5) to their audience (chapter 6). In the end, the student should ask the audience to make an investment (chapter 7) in getting to know them!

Follow-up Questions/Discussions

- Was it hard to promote yourself or easy?
- How much did you change your pitch thinking about who was your audience? Would a promo to a group of kids be different than one to your teacher next year? How and why?

Social Questions for Students

- We want to let the world know about ourselves, but how do we know the difference between being positive and bragging?
- How much is too much before we are being dishonest?

NOTE

1. Giving youth the tools to decide for themselves what products and ideas should be a part of their life harkens back to a slogan of the 1960s counterculture, a phrase that, if said by a young consumer, may be the best sign of a successful media literacy education: "Not with my life, you don't!"

Glossary

NOTE: Where possible, we have steered away from technical economic/financial definitions to assist the teacher in having an understanding that he can then pass on to his students. Lessons that directly address the term appear in parentheses.

Ad hominem fallacy: When one argues not by addressing the issue but by attacking one's opponent or those who disagree with one's point of view, such as claiming they are biased, have a bad motive, or don't know enough.

Ambience: The atmosphere or "feel" of a place, such as being "fun" or "mysterious." (4I)

Aspirational buying/thinking: In terms of demographics, when consumers (usually younger ones) imitate, as best that they can, the lifestyle and consumption habits of older consumers. (5E)

Bandwagon effect: The psychological nudge to do (or consume) something because others are doing it (such as by **peer pressure**). Also known as FOMO (Fear of Missing Out). (5D, 5G)

Barter system: A nonmonetary system of payment in which goods and services are exchanged for other goods and services. (3E)

Behavioral economics: A branch of economic study that examines the psychological factors on human decision making, including nonrational and even irrational motivations.

Brand impression: When a potential consumer sees or interacts with a product or its brand the cumulative effect of each encounter leads to a familiarity and thus positive feeling toward the product, leading to a desire to consume it or at least choose that brand over others. (4B)

Buyer's remorse: A feeling of regret ("I shouldn't have done that") a buyer feels after a purchase, often because the buyer thinks the product was not worth the price or that there was a better use for what was spent. (8K)

Centrics: Core needs or desires of a particular demographic group that can be appealed to in order to nudge a potential consumer to consume a good or service.

Confirmation bias: The tendency to interpret data, a message, or a situation as being aligned with or supporting the interpreter's already established conclusions or beliefs. (9B)

Conspicuous consumption: Overtly consuming a good or service so that one may gain panache from others seeing the consumption as a status privilege. (5B)

Consumer sovereignty: The theory that a producer/consumer (seller/buyer) market is driven more by the desires and demands of the consumers, with producers responding to those desires. The buyer calls the tune; the band plays to suit the listeners' wants.

Context: Understanding something (including its meaning) by considering the words and circumstances surrounding its use, like "Oh, please!" being used nicely or sarcastically. (9G, 9H)

Coolhunting: Actively seeking out new or rising trends (often by observing people perceived as trendsetters).

Cost-benefit analysis: The primary method of decision making in economics, whereby a person weighs (consciously or subconsciously) both the advantages and disadvantages of one option against another. (3F)

Currency: A form of money generally accepted as acceptable payment within a community. (3E)

Data: Information drawn from measurement or observation (often from controlled experiments) that is then used to draw conclusions. Contrary to what many say, data itself "tells" a person nothing. It is the interpretation and analysis of data from which one draws conclusions, with such conclusions being only as good as both the data and the analysis are in combination.

Diminishing return, law of: When a consumer receives less benefit or enjoyment (**utility**) out of a good or service acquired despite **investing** (putting in) the same amount of resources or cost to acquire that good or service previously; in casual economics (or layman's) terms, not getting the same bang for the buck one used to. (3G)

Economist: A person who studies the process and resulting choices that individuals and large groups make as to the use of resources, especially **scarce** ones. It's most associated with choices about money, but any decision as to how to use something (such as time or attention) one does not have enough of to do all one wishes is an economic choice.

Editorial: An article written more with an intent to give the writer's opinion or views on a topic than to present objective news or information on it. (9D)

Ergonomics: Designing products and systems to be most efficient (including comfort, usability, mastery) for human use. (4E)

Ethos appeal: A method of trying to persuade people to accept information or messaging because of the authority, credibility, or appeal of the speaker. Also called an endorsement. (4C)

External honorific booty: A good or service whose utility comes from conspicuous consumption, or other people seeing and admiring the consumption as a privilege of status. (5B)

Factors of production: The **resources** that go into making or producing a good, usually subdivided into land (raw materials), labor (work force), and capital (tools, machines, and money). (3B, 3C)

Fads: Intense, temporary interest or popularity in a product or activity, leading to a rush in consumption due to the **bandwagon effect**. (5D)

Fallacy: An argument based on unsound reasoning or improper factors.

Feedback loop: A phenomenon whereby media, reporting a purported trend, inspire consumers to follow the trend (due to the **bandwagon effect**), which then seemingly confirms the initial report. Often a starting point for **fads**. (9B)

GRAIL: An acronym for five major demographic attributes of consumers: Gender, Race, Age, Income, and Lifestyle.

Hasty generalization/conclusion: A fallacy whereby a conclusion is drawn from insufficient evidence, often utilized to ascribe a characteristic of a few or some members of a group to all its members (from an insufficient sample size). (4F, 9E)

Honorific booty: Goods or services acquired more for the psychological **utility** (good feeling) of possessing it rather than practical **utility**. (5A, 5B)

Implied messaging, implication: Suggesting a statement through indirect words, images, or actions without directly stating the message. (9F, 9G)

Inflation: When the price of goods rises because there is greater demand (and therefore money offered) than there are available goods, or because the money used to pay for things is considered of less value, so a seller demands more of it. (3E)

Information: Facts or data presented without motive or bias, as opposed to **persuasion**.

Internal honorific booty: A good or service whose **utility** comes from the good feeling the consumer has from possessing/utilizing it, regardless of whether others know, such as a keepsake. (5A)

Investment (money or time): An outlay (payment) of goods, money, or one's time and effort in anticipation of a delayed but greater return (payment) in the future, called a **return on investment**. (8I, 8J, 8K)

KGOY (Kids Getting Older Younger): The idea that children today are exposed to and are aware of facets of society, including marketing and consumption, earlier in life than previous generations, implied that it's to a negative psychological effect and leads to **aspirational thinking**. (8E)

Logo: A picture or graphic design used by a company to instantly bring that company to a viewer's mind. (4J)

Logos appeal: A method of trying to persuade people to accept information or messaging because of logic or rational factors such as data. (9I)

Marginal utility: The benefit (such as satisfaction) a consumer gets from consuming or utilizing one *additional* unit of a good or service, such as the amount of thirst quenched by drinking an additional soda. Distinguished from **return on investment**, as **ROI** is the gain one gained from something already consumed. (3G)

Market penetration: The amount (such as percentage of population) a product is consumed within a particular **niche** or demographic group. (8D)

Media literacy: The ability to critically evaluate, understand, and decode messages to discern the difference between **information** and **persuasion**, to see what is both explicitly and implicitly messaged, for the consumer of information ultimately to have more control of the diet of messaging they consume.

Medium of exchange: Something, such as money, that acts as a middle or common reference point (such as value) in purchasing goods and services.

Monetary value: Whether a good is deemed to have **utility** based on how much other consumers would pay for it. (5A)

Negative honorific booty: A good or service whose **utility** comes from society's perceiving such consumption as a negative or rebellious act, lending to the consumer's **panache** for being independent or a rebel.

Niche: That part of the general population of potential buyers (**GRAIL**) wherein a product will sell well, and thus the consumers to whom a seller should pitch his or her goods. (6A)

Nonrational factors on decision making: Factors (often emotional or visceral) beyond traditional factors of price, quality, and availability, which may be weighed in economic decision making.

Norm: A behavior or belief that is seen as the standard, accepted, and proper one of a society, with behaviors or beliefs contrary to the norm being unusual, socially deviant, or even possibly morally wrong. (7D)

Nudge/nudging: As conceived of by Richard Thaler, any factor that alters people's behavior in a predictable way without forbidding any options or significantly changing their economic incentives.

Panache: Having a style or manner, usually indicating superior socioeconomic status, that stands out and is admired by others; coolness.

Pathos appeal: A method of trying to persuade people to accept information or messaging because of emotion (such as sympathy). (9I)

Glossary

Pecuniary emulation: When consumers imitate, as best that they can, the consumption habits of those in higher socioeconomic statuses in an attempt to gain **panache**.

Peer pressure: A kind of **bandwagon effect** where a person is **nudged** to do something (or avoid something) so as to fit in (or not stand out) from people like them. It is social pressure to behave a certain way, believe something, or consume something because others around you do it, whether or not you like it. (5G, 5H)

Persuasion: The act of presenting information with intent to affect the receiver's opinion, belief, or point of view, such as in an **editorial**. (9D)

Preconception: A view or opinion of something before one encounters it. Can lead to **confirmation bias**. (9E)

Rare goods (rarity): Goods that there are few of, regardless of demand. (3D)

Resources: The things used to make other things. They can be generally divided into categories, called **factors of production**, and can be concrete (wood to make a chair) or abstract (the skill or time it takes to fashion the wood into the chair). The resources themselves may be made up of resources that helped make them. (3B, 3C)

Return on investment (ROI): The gain or good one gets from using something over and above the thing's original value. It implies more of an investment gamble than **marginal utility** and may be tangible (like interest earned) or intangible (the joy and fun of using it). Paying $10 for a movie one is not sure about depletes one of $10, but the ROI is the entertainment of the two hours watching, along with any happy remembrances of the movie or outing. (8J)

Sampling error: When a tester draws incorrect or improper conclusions because the people or subjects observed (sample size) did not accurately reflect the larger group. (4F, 6B)

Scarce goods (scarcity): Goods that there are fewer of than demand for it (i.e., more people want it than there are units of it available). (3A, 3D, 3E)

Sentimental value: The value of something based on a person's emotional attachment to it rather than its money worth on the market. (5A)

Social science: The scientific study of humans and human relationships (as opposed to physical sciences that study physical phenomena), using scientific methods to observe, quantify, and draw conclusions. (2A)

Stalagmite effect: A phenomenon whereby incremental changes accumulate to form a significant effect over time, as stalagmites are created from drops of calcite over many years. (6D)

Stereotype: A generalization made about a larger population based upon a few (and not enough) members. (4F, 6B)

Teaching format—Circle talk: A classroom style generally composed of students exchanging ideas through discussion; generally more open and free-form, allowing students more time and space to discuss.

Teaching format—Fishbowl: A classroom style generally composed of a fast-paced, rotating participatory technique designed to promote a more quickly evolving discussion than a **circle talk** format.

Teaching format—Improv: A classroom style generally composed of giving students a prompt or setup that they must act out, incorporating extraneous elements or information after a short (or no) preparation time.

Teaching format—Socratic seminar: A classroom style wherein students focus on discussing guided questions; more formal than **circle talk** but more open than a **fishbowl** format.

Tells: Inadvertent behavior or mannerism that reveals the person's intent, meaning, or even honesty. (10A)

Trade-off: The act of making a choice as between two or more things or actions when one can't have (or, in the case of messaging, believe) both. This involves a comparison of the plusses and minuses of choosing each option, called a **cost-benefit analysis**. (3F)

Utility: The benefit or usefulness a consumer gets from having and using a good, whether tangible (food as nutrition), personal (the comfort feeling of a particular food), or esoteric (the admiration of others from eating certain foods).

Viral advertising: A marketing technique whereby marketers use consumers (or apparent consumers) to market products, often through social networks. (4B)

Visceral processing: Responding to information based on inward ("gut") feelings rather than logic or reasoning. (9I)

Bibliography

Crain, Caleb. "Why We Don't Read, Revisited." *The New Yorker*. June 14, 2018. https://www.newyorker.com/culture/cultural-comment/why-we-dont-read-revisited.

Henry, Holly K. M., and Dina L. G. Borzekowski. *The Nag Factor: How Do Children Convince Their Parents to Buy Unhealthy Foods?* Johns Hopkins University Bloomberg School of Public Health. August 11, 2011. https://www.jhsph.edu/news/news-releases/2011/borzekowski-nag-factor.html.

Krasniak, Michelle. "Visual Content and Social Media Marketing: New Research." *Social Media Examiner*. May 30, 2017. https://www.socialmediaexaminer.com/visual-content-and-social-media-marketing-new-research/.

Levitt, Steven D., and Stephen J. Dubner. *Freakonomics: A Rogue Economist Explores the Hidden Side of Everything*. New York: William Morrow, 2005.

Malabrigo, Victoria. "Visual Content on Social Media: 2017 Trends and Research." WNET/New York Public Media Interactive Engagement Group. March 13, 2017, https://ieg.wnet.org/2017/03/visual-content-social-media-2017-trends-research/.

McNeal, James U. *Kids as Customers: A Handbook of Marketing to Children*. New York: Lexington Books, 1992.

Ruskin, Gary. "Why They Whine: How Corporations Prey on Our Children." *Mothering Magazine*. July 1, 2003. http://www.mothering.com/10-0-0/html/10-3-0/10-3-whine97.shtml.

Siegel, David, Timothy Coffey, and Gregory Livingston. *The Great Tween Buying Machine: Marketing to Today's Tweens*. Ithaca, NY: Paramount Market Publishing, 2001.

Thaler, Richard, and Cass Sunstein. *Nudge: Improving Decisions about Health, Wealth and Happiness*. New York: Penguin Books, 2009.

Veblen, Thorstein. *The Theory of the Leisure Class*. New York: Macmillan, 1899.

Wasserman, Jim, and David Loveland. "More than Reality." *American School Board Journal* 204, no. 2 (April 2017).

About the Authors

Jim Wasserman has had two career lives: first as a business litigation attorney and then, for twenty-five years, as a humanities teacher specializing in media literacy. Jim was a pioneer in teaching and developing curricula regarding media literacy in secondary schools, starting as far back as the 1990s (when he, ironically, had to explain social networking to teens!). Jim has also been willing to throw himself into the media mix to better understand the Brave New World of media—from being an early adopter of social media, to publishing articles over the past thirty years on subjects ranging from law, to finance, to education, even appearing with his wife on (and winning!) a national reality game show. Jim now lives in Granada, Spain, where he writes articles on behavioral economics and media literacy and, with his wife, maintains a blog (http://yourthirdlife.com) on the financial, logistical, and lifestyle aspects of retiring overseas. Jim had dreamed of leading an Ernest Hemingway–like writer's life in Spain, though the closest he has come so far is becoming a personal attendant to a host of cats.

Dave Loveland is a middle-school humanities teacher who has spent his career engaging his students in creative, cooperative, and critical activities such as Model Congress and Mock Trial to place them in the role of civic participant rather than simple observer. His professional goal is to use lessons from American history to give context and make sense of today's headlines. As media becomes more inundated with all kinds of dubious and contradictory information, Dave can most often be heard telling his students to check their research and go back to the source. He loves telling the stories of history and igniting a passion in his students to learn more about the world, the people in it, and themselves.

Dave and Jim, together, have published articles on education and media, which have been featured in education journals from America to Australia.

www.ingramcontent.com/pod-product-compliance
Ingram Content Group UK Ltd.
Pitfield, Milton Keynes, MK11 3LW, UK
UKHW040203230326
469204UK00001B/24